ONE
MORNING
IN JULY

ONE MORNING IN JULY

The Man Who Was First on the Scene Tells His Story
About the Day That Changed London Forever

Aaron Debnam

JOHN BLAKE

Published by John Blake Publishing Ltd,
3 Bramber Court, 2 Bramber Road,
London W14 9PB, England

www.blake.co.uk

First published in hardback in 2007

ISBN 978 1 84454 449 3

British Library Cataloguing-in-Publication Data:

A catalogue record for this book is available from the British Library.

Design by www.envydesign.co.uk

Printed and bound in Great Britain by William Clowes Ltd, Beccles,
Suffolk

1 3 5 7 9 10 8 6 4 2

Papers used by John Blake Publishing are natural, recyclable
products made from wood grown in sustainable forests.
The manufacturing processes conform to the environmental
regulations of the country of origin.

Every attempt has been made to contact the relevant copyright-holders,
but some were unobtainable. We would be grateful if the appropriate
people could contact us.

PREFACE

I think before I start recounting the events of 7 July 2005, I should talk a little about why I am writing this book and what motivated me to do it. I know that this is a very sensitive issue for a lot of people for a variety of reasons, so I am very mindful of how I want this book to be received and interpreted.

This is not just a story about me, but an account of the actions of everyone I worked with that day. It is a tale of the heroism of the emergency services and the bravery of the victims who had been trapped after the explosion on the Piccadilly Line tube train between Kings Cross and Russell Square. I want people to understand that the story of that day did not end when the all clear was given and the survivors were taken off the train – its effects are still being felt today by everyone who was directly involved, and always will be.

In the book you are about to read, I have written about the proceedings of that day in as much detail as I can, but I have been careful not to go into too much detail in certain areas. I am very aware that 26 people did not get off that train and all of those had family and friends that may read this book. I have strived to be as respectful as I can while still trying to convey the impact that those dreadful scenes had on me at the time.

I have written about the confusion and the chaos surrounding the situation, but also of the amazing things achieved by the emergency services on the day – not just by the individuals on the ground but also by the organisations as a whole. They managed to coordinate a massive deployment of people power and control over four separate major incidents, any of which would have been chaotic enough on its own.

For over a year now, I have been struggling with the psychological scars that my experiences have left me with and it has been the same for many people that were involved, whether they were members of the emergency services, one of the day's casualties or family members of a victim. My main hope for this book is that I can raise awareness of the effects that can beset the human mind when it has experienced a traumatic event. I have been through what I can only describe as a living hell trying to come to terms with the residual effects of that day and I feel an almost overpowering urge to try and make people understand what that is like. Just because you cannot see a psychological injury that does not mean it is any less real than a physical one.

Since that awful day, I have come into contact with people who did not appreciate this and – through no fault of theirs – life was made very difficult for me. It is those people that I most want to reach. If I can make people see that post-traumatic stress disorder is a very real condition, then perhaps they will recognise the symptoms in someone else and save them some of the anguish that I had to endure.

I hope that this book is received not as just an account of one day's events but as a piece of a story that is still going on – an explanation of the fact that the people involved are not just names on a news programme but real people who have been left to rebuild their lives after it had been changed drastically by the actions of others. None of us asked to be there on that day, but all of us have been forced to deal with the effects of it. This is my way of trying to do that.

Writing this book has been a real journey for me. I have always been a very private person and you will see as you read this that I do not share my feelings with many people. This is the first time that I have spoken about my experiences in any detail and it actually feels very strange for me to be doing it in this way. Even the people who are closest to me have not heard what is contained in these pages, but I feel that the story is too important for me to keep it inside any longer.

When I started writing, I never expected it to turn out the way that it did. I was just recording my experiences for my own peace of mind. But now I know that people are going to read this book, I hope that everyone can take away a little something from it. That will make it all just a little more worthwhile and make the risks of opening up my heart on these pages a little easier to face.

Aaron Debnam
Whitstable, Kent 2007

ACKNOWLEDGEMENTS

I would like to thank the people who have been supportive throughout the production of this book:

The British Transport Police, especially my colleagues Gary, Ray and Glenn, and Anne and Derek from the occupational health team.

The NHS Trauma Stress Clinic, especially Jenny.

John Blake Publishing – John, Rosie, Clive and Michelle.

Claire Sawford.

The two people who encouraged me to have this published, Gill Hicks and Joe Kerr.

And finally, but not least, the woman who is beside me each day, Flo.

CONTENTS

Chapter One

THE CALL:
7 JULY 2005

I can remember the events of that morning as clearly as if they had happened to me yesterday – in fact, I think that they will be etched into my memory for the rest of my life. It was an experience so profound that it had an effect on nearly every aspect of my life for the following year and I have no doubt that it has changed me fundamentally as a person forever.

It was just a normal shift for me, an early turn. Basically, that means I would have been up since the disgusting time of four in the morning to start the commute to work from my house in deepest, darkest Kent. I was pretty grumpy that morning. My boss had given me the unenviable task of doing the court run with the prisoners that were in the cells downstairs. I always found this job extremely boring, as it means that you are unavailable to take calls until the task is complete. There is nothing more frustrating than a really juicy job coming out over the radio that you can't attend because you have a prisoner in the back of the van. As per my normal routine when I have the hump, I went outside the station, hid in a corner and smoked for a while, until I was just late enough to let people know that I was not happy. I never said I wasn't childish.

Working with me that morning was an older officer by the name of Gary. Gary doesn't really need an excuse to be grumpy – he is grumpy about everything most of the time. I sometimes think that being grumpy actually makes Gary happy, and if nothing had happened that had pissed him off then he would go and look for something. That said, working with Gary was probably the highlight of my day – he is a great bloke. His dry nature makes me chuckle quietly to myself for the majority of the shift and, as an added bonus, he is one of my smoking buddies. Looking back, I cannot think of another officer I would have rather worked with on that day.

Gary and I walked into the custody suite at our station about an hour after we were briefed. I can't give you exact timings for that day – things went so suddenly from being mundane and boring to being completely mental that I do not even remember looking at my watch until after everything was over. We were waiting around in there for what seemed like an age, the custody sergeants and the jailers had just taken over from the night shift and were preparing the prisoners for court and getting them fed. So Gary and I smoked some more, Gary moaned about the wait and I dutifully listened. I wasted some time backing the van into the yard so that as soon as the first prisoner was ready I could get on with the job in hand as quickly as possible and get him to court for his case to be heard.

It was just before nine o'clock, I think, when the first call came out that gave me the impression that it was all going to go tits up. I was half listening to my personal radio and I just caught the end of a transmission – '... EXPLOSION LIVERPOOL STREET'. This, as you can imagine, got me fully engaged and I turned my set up so that the whole of custody could hear it. The transmission repeated in full: 'ANY UNITS TO ATTEND LIVERPOOL STREET, REPORT OF AN EXPLOSION IN THE UNDERGROUND, ANY UNIT TO ATTEND?' Everybody in the custody suite stopped what they were doing to listen in and I remember turning to Gary and saying to him that we should forget the prisoners and get down there. Gary, being more experienced and a little calmer in just about everything he does, said we should wait. I listened as more and more units put themselves up for the call and became increasingly frustrated with being stuck where I was. Several minutes later, the control room asked on the radio for the duty officer to attend the scene of the suspected incident and I immediately saw this as my ticket to the show.

The duty officer on the day was an inspector called Glen, known to us as 'the Governor'. He had been my direct boss for the last year of my service and I feel that I need to tell you a little bit about him before I go on. I remember the first time I met Glen – it was at the leaving party for my old inspector in a pub near Warren Street Tube Station. He was dressed as your stereotypical ex-public schoolboy: he had the mad hair, the thick-rimmed glasses with the tatty suit jacket, a bad T-shirt, and a tatty old pair of running shoes. You might be thinking that this combination of clothing may be a little trendy on a young student on a night out in the West End, but you have to believe me when I say that Glen is no 20-year-old student.

He came and spoke to me and other members of the team during the course of the evening and we all felt after meeting him that he was a really nice guy. Over the course of the next year, I came to know Glen quite well. I knew him to be a very relaxed supervisor, as long as his bosses were leaving him alone, and when all was well he basically left us alone to do our job with very little interference. You do not get to the rank of inspector without knowing your stuff and being able to deal with every aspect of any incident that you are likely to attend.

I heard Glen on the radio requesting transport to the scene and before Gary could even think about stopping me I had offered our services. Glen was in the same building as us, so I pulled the van round the front while Gary went upstairs to get him. All the while, I could hear the radio traffic coming from the scene and there was clearly a great deal of confusion about what had happened. The original call was for an explosion, but in the space of a couple of minutes it had turned into an electrical failure. I suspect now that this information had come from the people at London Underground as they can monitor the traction current that powers the trains from their control room. If the explosion had severed the tracks, then that is the first thing that would have alerted them that there was a problem. No one on the scene seemed to have the first idea of what was going on and to me, listening in from the outside, it sounded like pandemonium.

Gary and Glen came outside a couple of minutes later; Gary jumped in the back of the van and Glen sat in the passenger seat next to me. I had just come off my specialist police-driving course and this was only about my fifth drive with the siren and blue flashing lights – the 'blues and twos' – so I was pretty nervous with the boss on board, as you can imagine. I set off at quite a pace – I could sense the urgency of the call by the radio traffic and I just wanted to get there as soon as possible. There were now reports of passengers emerging from the tunnel at Liverpool Street and Aldgate stations covered in black soot, some with minor injuries. My mind was racing; I was trying to drive as fast as I could through the rush-hour traffic and listen to my radio at the same time. Reports kept coming in, but the information was sketchy, confused and sometimes conflicting. The traffic was really bad – it felt like the whole of London was trying to stop us getting to our destination.

I had decided that I would go the most direct route to the City and then wing it from there. I do not know that part of London well – the medieval street layout of the area resembles a rabbit warren more than the heart of our nation's capital. I sped down the City Road at speeds that would make a Formula One driver nervous; being on the wrong side of the road for most of the journey just added to the excitement of it all. I went into the City off the Old Street roundabout, but I was pretty lost from this point. I found myself relying on the ridiculously small road signs they have in the City, which are designed for pedestrian tourists rather than speeding police transit vans. But, eventually, I shot past a sign with the British Rail logo on it and took the next left turn.

Chapter Two

LIVERPOOL STREET

I ended up at the back of Liverpool Street Station, by the taxi rank, but the front of the station had been broadcast as the rendezvous for the emergency services. The Governor decided that he would jump out of the van in the taxi rank and make his way round on foot while I found a place to park the van so that I could join him at the scene later. Glen jumped out, but I had completely forgotten about Gary. In my haste to get stuck in I floored the van, completely oblivious to the fact that Gary was half in and half out of the sliding door at the side of the van. I heard him cry out and instinctively put on the brakes. I had only gone a couple of feet, but I could tell it had put the fear of God into my mate Gaz. The look on his face was a classic and he flew at me with every swear word in his vocabulary – which, by the way, is extensive. If any member of the public had been watching us at the time, it would have looked like a *Carry On* film. I couldn't help but laugh to myself, but I think that it was out of nervousness and shock rather than because I found the situation funny. Anyway, Gary shut the door after another torrent of abuse directed at me and I drove off, leaving a very disgruntled police constable in my wake.

I drove out onto the main road; the traffic was at an absolute standstill. The emergency services had shut off Bishopsgate, and this was having a major knock-on effect on the whole of the city. The road was split in the middle by a concrete barrier that prevented me from going on the other side of the road, so I was forced to drive with two wheels on the pavement and two on the road. It took what seemed like an age to go just two hundred yards. I could see the police cordon that had been put in place in one of the side roads leading to the station and that was what I aimed for.

Eventually I got there and pulled into a scene that I do not think I will ever see again. As far as emergency services were concerned, the world and his wife were there. I have never seen so many police, ambulance crew and firemen in my life. Everyone was trying to clear members of the public from the surrounding buildings and the street and impose some semblance of order.

An inspector from the City of London police was trying to control the situation. He had established a cordon and was directing the people power that he had to where it was needed. He spotted me in my van and instructed me to pull it across the junction to block any vehicle from entering the closed-off area. I did as I was asked, but I positioned the van just in time to block three fire engines from entering the scene. After being shouted at by a fire officer in a white helmet I tried to move the van, but stalled it, as I was flapping a bit by this point. It had taken me about seven minutes to drive from the West End of London to the centre of the City and my adrenaline was through the roof. I seriously needed to calm down and I seriously needed a cigarette.

When I finally let the fire engines pass and had my van back in position, I started to get a grip on myself. I had hidden in the back of the van for a few minutes, satisfied my dirty habit and was ready to face the world again with a fresh hit of nicotine in my system. I got out of the van and started to take in the scene, trying to work out what was happening, but the radio traffic was still very confused and the incident was still being treated as a major power outage. At this point, I saw two officers I knew standing on the cordon. I went over to them to see if they were more clued-up than I was about the situation. One of the officers was a man called Guy, and I knew him quite well. He had been on my shift for a few months and was working that day with an officer by the name of John, who was guesting on our team that morning.

Guy had taken an early call to Liverpool Street that morning and told me that he was the person who had put out the original call for the explosion. He explained that he and John had been in the underground station dealing with a minor incident when they had heard – and felt – a massive explosion coming from the Tube network beneath them. He said that they had gone down on to the platform and that the place had been filled with smoke; there were people

9

streaming out of the tunnels covered in soot. The two officers had made their way back upstairs to put out the emergency call and had waited there for reinforcements. But when other officers had started to arrive, Guy and John were ordered to deal with crowd control and eventually ended up on the cordon. I could tell by the tone of Guy's voice that he was disappointed with this as he is a very hands-on person, and if there were to be a rescue he would have wanted to be involved.

A few minutes had passed and I was starting to resign myself to the fact that I would be stuck on the cordon for the duration of the incident. There was still no sign of the Governor or Gary, so I started directing the public and trying to keep the area clear for the emergency services to work in. People were asking me a lot of questions about what was happening, but I couldn't tell them as – frustratingly – I didn't know the answers any more than they did.

Ten minutes must have passed before the next odd call came out on the radio. I remember it exactly: 'ANY UNIT TO ATTEND EDGWARE ROAD UNDERGROUND STATION FOR A PERSON UNDER A TRAIN.' This situation was now getting really strange. A person under a train is exactly what it sounds like: someone has jumped, been pushed or fallen under a moving train. At first I thought that it must be a coincidence, but the more I thought about it the more it just felt wrong. It wasn't until later that day that I learned the person struck by the train had been blown out of a window from a carriage in which a bomb had exploded, directly into the path of a train going in the other direction.

A short time later, I heard Glen on the radio – his call sign was Lima Tango Eight. He was offering to attend Edgware Road, as a supervisor is needed at an incident of that nature, and I remember thinking that it was a good thing as I'd rather be busy than standing around directing traffic. His offer was taken up and I prepared myself and the van to go. I radioed him my position and he was there a minute later with Gary in tow. We all boarded the van once again and I went back the way I came to get back into the West End with the lights and sirens blaring. The drive was even worse this time: the traffic had been building up all the time we were at Liverpool Street and it was now gridlocked. Radio traffic was still very heavy and the situation we had just left was starting to make sense. Officers had been down into the tunnel and had encountered a train with what they described as bomb damage. This suddenly made the reality of the situation absolutely clear: for the first time, we knew that we were dealing with a terrorist attack of some description. And for the first time, I started to doubt that we were attending a routine incident at Edgware Road.

As I got out of the City, the call for units to attend King's Cross was broadcast. We were committed to a call and there were already dozens of units on their way to the Cross, so we continued without deviation. But as we reached the Euston Road and started heading towards the A40, another message was put out on the radio. This one, too, is branded into my memory: 'ANY UNIT IN THE VICINITY AVAILABLE TO ATTEND RUSSELL SQUARE LU STATION, REPORTS OF NUMEROUS WALKING WOUNDED AT THAT

LOCATION.' I remember thinking, 'Shit, we are right on top of it.' I turned to Glen in the passenger seat and told him that we had to go. Gary was giving him similar sentiments from the back. Glen took a second to consider his options and as there were already several units going to Edgware, he told me to turn around and drive to the latest call.

I cannot explain properly the way I was feeling at the time. It seemed like the whole world had gone mad and that we were running round in circles chasing our tails. Calls were going out all over the place and confusion was rife. My adrenaline was up, I had driven from one end of London to the other then back again on the blues and twos and now I was heading into the unknown. My story so far may sound a little confused, but that's because it was. It wasn't until later that I knew exactly what I needed to do and how I was going to do it.

The route to Russell Square from the Euston Road is easy to navigate on a normal day, but this – as we have already established – was not one of those. The road was completely jammed with traffic and for sections of the drive I was completely on the pavement. I had to squeeze that van through gaps so tight that the Governor and I had to push the wing mirrors out again after I had negotiated each one. I drove down a couple of one-way streets in the wrong direction and literally threw the *Highway Code* out of the window in order to make some progress. The time from us receiving the call to us arriving at the station was no more than four minutes and we were the first police to arrive.

Chapter Three

FIRST ON
THE SCENE

The point at which we arrived at the station is still a little hazy in my memory; the magnitude of the scene that we were initially confronted with was staggering. The entire entrance to the station was full of wounded commuters. Most were just suffering from smoke inhalation and were covered in black soot, but there were others who were suffering from what seemed like flying-glass injuries. All of them looked like they had been through hell and it really took me aback. There were several members of the public and members of the station's staff administering first aid to some of the wounded, but most seemed to be wandering around in a daze. I would estimate that there were at least one hundred and fifty people in the station's booking hall and immediately outside in the street.

Glen led Gary and me into the station; we made our way

through the crowds and I think that the Governor was looking for someone who could shed some light on the situation. We got through the ticket barriers and the crowd started to thin out. In this area there were some more seriously injured people with more extensive glass injuries; most were lying on the floor, staring at the ceiling in a state of total shock. I can remember one woman sitting up against the wall, covered up to her neck in a blanket or a big coat. She seemed to be staring right at me, but when I tried to talk to her I realised that she was actually staring straight through me, oblivious to all going on around her. I thought at that moment, 'What the fuck has she seen that would mess her up like that?'

As we approached the back of the station by the lifts that lead down to the platforms, we were met by a man who I initially thought worked for the Underground. I cannot remember his name, but was told afterwards that he worked for Network Rail or Railtrack and had come to help out from an office building down the road; he was very dirty and had clearly been to the scene below. He started talking to the Governor, but to tell the truth I really didn't listen to what was said. I was too busy trying to fathom my surroundings and had phased out of reality for a short while. I was looking around at the scene and thinking, 'If it's this bad up here, then what can it possibly be like under the ground?'

It wasn't long before I was snapped out of my little trance. Glen had made the decision to go down to the platform and see what the situation was like down there. He asked me to radio for more officers and ambulances to attend our location, as the three of us were clearly going to need help. With that done, we started our descent to the southbound Piccadilly Line. We were forced to take the spiral staircase down to the platforms as the power was out and the lifts were not working. I loathe doing that at the best of times: I hate heights and enclosed spaces, so there is nothing I dislike more than descending 250 feet into a tunnel system. I always get a bit panicky when I have to do it and I consciously have to steady myself every time.

When we reached the bottom, the Railtrack guy led the way onto the platform and again I was shocked by what confronted us. The first thing that hit me was the heat. I have spent a lot of time on the Tube system in all conditions, but I have never felt it that hot before or since. I started to sweat almost instantly; it felt like it sauna. Next I noticed the smell, one that will not leave me for the rest of my days. It smelt like burning hair but the air was thick with it, so that you could taste it. It made me feel sick to my stomach and for days afterwards I could smell it on my skin no matter how much I scrubbed myself. There was also a lot of smoke in the air; it gave everything a very hazy quality that made the whole thing seem even more surreal. With the smoke, the heat and the smell combined, it was already hard to breathe normally; all I could think of was what it would be like in the tunnel. I noticed all of these things in a heartbeat because I was also surrounded by some very seriously wounded people. There were not as many as there were upstairs, but these were obviously the ones who could not make the climb or could not be moved.

A team of paramedics had arrived at some point and all three of them were working on separate casualties. I remember that there was one man sitting on one of the wooden benches on the platform. He was filthy dirty, the same as everyone else, but I could tell that he was as white as a sheet under all the grime. His lips were blue and he was shaking uncontrollably. It looked like he had lost an eye, or at least sustained a very serious injury to that area of his face, and a young paramedic was talking to him, trying to calm him down. I also remember another man lying on the floor. Another paramedic was working on him and he had the worst injury that I had seen so far. One of his feet was missing from the ankle down and he was covered in blood and the ever-present black soot. I found it strange looking at him because he wasn't making a sound; like the others upstairs, he was just staring at the ceiling like his body had shut down to protect itself from the horror that the day had brought. Another thing that I found strange was the way he was dressed: he was wearing a very nice three-piece suit and was obviously a businessman of some description. I found myself thinking that he had probably made the same journey hundreds of times before, he may have had no trouble with it in the past apart from the odd late Tube train. Why should today be unlike any other?

I really couldn't look at these poor souls any more; I felt so helpless, but I knew that there was nothing that I could have done for them. I knew that the people who really needed our help were still on the train somewhere in the darkness of that tunnel. I turned back to the Governor, who was in a bit of a meeting with some station staff on the platform and the Railtrack guy; the latter was obviously the most clued-up person about the situation. They were discussing going down the tunnel, but I got the impression that Glen wanted to wait for more people to arrive so that we would have enough hands for the work that lay ahead.

I started to switch on a little now. I had been a bit stunned by the extreme environment that I had found myself in and with all the previous excitement of the day I think I had become a little overwhelmed. I started to consider what we would need for the wounded in the tunnel, the things that were available to us at that moment in that place. I was dripping with sweat by now, so I took off my body armour and laid it to one side. I kept my utility belt on, though, because it contained my torch and other items that I knew I might need in the immediate future.

The first thing that I thought about was some kind of liquid. I didn't know how long those people had been in the tunnel but if there were any left alive then they would need to have something to drink. The only source of liquid that I could find on the platform was a soft-drink vending machine, I asked a member of staff if he had a key, but he said that he did not and didn't know who had. So there was only one thing for it and that was to smash it open. I took my metal baton out of my belt and extended it to its full length. These are quite heavy pieces of equipment and have a large counterweight on the end that you grip. Using this counterweight, I started to lay in to the machine. It had a glass front, but the thing was tougher than it looked. I don't know how long I was smashing it for, but it must have been a while. I could feel people gathering around me as I was working myself into a frenzy. But all the effort was in vain as when I finally got through the toughened glass I found a steel plate behind it. It was clear that the liquid we needed was not coming from this source. The vending machine had served one purpose though, and that was to distract me for a few minutes. It stopped me worrying about what lay ahead of us, and while I had been smashing away another half a dozen police officers had arrived.

I met back up with Gaz, whom I had lost track of for a while. We stood chatting at the entrance to the tunnel, but all the while I could feel myself getting a little agitated. I'm not the world's most patient person at my best, and I really felt that we had wasted enough time on the platform and needed to get to the people still in the tunnel. I said as much to Gary, who replied in his usual calm manner that I should wait for Glen to make his decision. This had no effect on me and I started to pace up and down and work myself up. I was sure that we had enough people to go down and I couldn't understand the wait. As I looked up the platform, all I could see were people standing around having a discussion. I snapped, and shouted, 'For fuck's sake, Guv, come on!' I know now that Glen was doing the right thing. He was making sure that he had considered every possible option available to him before we went into the tunnel. He was the officer in charge at the scene and was directly responsible for the lives of every person there.

It may have been what I said, or he may have simply decided that the time was right, but he finally gave the nod for us to start down the tunnel. I picked up some first-aid equipment that I had gathered and jumped down onto the tracks.

Chapter Four

THE TUNNEL

The Railtrack guy led the way, I was directly behind him with the paramedics, and the rest followed. There were about twelve of us in total. I remember the guy leading telling us not to touch the tracks as it was not confirmed whether the power was off or not. As you would expect, the tunnel was very dark, and with only the emergency lighting and our torches to see by it was a very oppressive place to be.

I have already said that I am very claustrophobic, so I was not having the time of my life down there. I had never been in a Tube tunnel before and did not realise there might be obstacles on the floor just waiting to trip you up in the dark. The left-hand side of the tunnel was carpeted with equipment between the rails that made the going really hard.

It was hotter in the tunnel and the smoke was much thicker. It seemed that with every step we took it became harder to breathe. The female paramedic told us to breathe through our noses, I think the better to help us filter out the dust and smoke, but it was so hard to breathe that this proved impossible. I was really sweating by now; it was soaking my clothes and running down my legs into my boots. It is very hard to describe how horrible the conditions were down there, but the air felt thick, as if you almost had to wade through it, and the farther in we went the worse it got. I'm not sure how long we were walking for, but it seemed like an age. All the while, my mind was working on overdrive, so many questions were running through my head, none of which I had any answers to yet. Were there any people left alive? Was there another bomb? Was the tunnel going to collapse on us? Was there a fire? Where on the train was the explosion? Was the power still on? All this was on my mind and I consciously had to clear my thoughts, otherwise I probably would have turned around and gone back to the station.

To make things worse, we had no communication with the outside world. We have radios that work underground, but they only seem to work in the stations; in the tunnel, we were completely isolated. If we needed help or any equipment, it would have to be the case of sending a runner all that way back to the station.

Things were getting unbearable with the heat and smoke, and those awful smells were getting stronger. But one plus point came when I tripped up and accidentally put my hand on the live rail: that answered the power question pretty conclusively, I think. I kept walking, but just as I was starting to think that we could not go on because the smoke was too thick, the train appeared out of the gloom.

That image of the train is still very vivid for me; it was like the scene from a horror film. The train almost filled the entire tunnel but there was a seam of emergency light around the edge that silhouetted it in the dark. I was so transfixed by this image that I kept walking, oblivious to the fact that the paramedics had stopped. Once I noticed that I was on my own I looked back and saw that they were dealing with a casualty. There were people left alive. They had found a man; it looked like he had dragged himself off the train and about fifteen yards up the tracks. He was wedged against the wall of the tunnel and looked barely conscious. As I looked at him more closely, I could see that he had lost his right leg from the knee down. It was not the first amputation that I had seen, but given what had already happened that day I was already pretty freaked out and this just exacerbated the feeling. I knew I would be seeing more of this – and worse – before the day was out. The paramedics worked on him for a short while and then some of the officers that were at the back of our party were tasked to carry him back to the station. We turned back towards the carriage and prepared ourselves to get on board.

Chapter Five

THE TRAIN

The paramedics were the first on. I stood and watched them climb the metal steps in the middle of the train and enter the driver's compartment. At this point, I froze. I honestly thought that I could not get on that train. I was scared that I couldn't deal with the scene that waited for me just at the top of those steps, and felt completely useless. I can't really say how long I stood there or how long it took me to think these things, because the next thing that I knew, I was in the train on the coat tails of the last paramedic. I am not proud that these thoughts entered my head, but at the end of the day I overcame my fears and did what was required of me when it mattered. I have no doubt in my mind that everyone who was with me, and the emergency services all over London, felt the same way at some point that day. I think that it is a natural reaction: you have to force your body to put itself into a position where you perceive a danger.

I entered that carriage and was stunned by the sight that greeted me. Never in my wildest imagination could I have pictured a scene of such complete devastation. Words escape me every time I try and describe what I saw there; none that I can think of could come close to doing it justice. I recognised the type of train instantly – I had been on a similar type thousands of times. It was one of the older ones – 1960s stock, I think – similar to the ones that run on the Victoria Line, which I use every day. But parts of the train were so damaged that they were unrecognisable. I could see immediately that there had been an explosion. There was a huge hole in the floor three-quarters of the way along the carriage and the ceiling was hanging down with all the wiring exposed. The sides of the train had been pushed out; they were flush to the side of the tunnel and there was hardly an intact window in sight. But all this was not the worst of it.

I am reluctant to talk about the human aspect of that scene. I am more than aware that the innocent victims on that train were the loved ones of people who might possibly read this and I feel guilty about revealing details of the people I saw there; it is as if I am violating their privacy. But I am writing this book to raise awareness about the horror of such incidents, so that people better understand the actions of the emergency services that attended and so those who, hopefully, will never experience an event such as this themselves can better understand the suffering of all the victims from that day.

THE TRAIN

The whole carriage was littered with what I can only describe as human debris. It was difficult to see the far end of the carriage because of the smoke and poor light, but I could see the silhouettes of bodies throughout its length. The far door of that first carriage, which connects it to the next, was damaged beyond recognition; it was hanging on by its hinges, but was crumpled like a piece of paper. It felt like time had stopped for me; I was still standing in the doorway that leads to the driver's compartment, but no one seemed to be moving. Nobody was ushering me farther onto the train and no one in front of me was moving deeper into the scene that we found ourselves in. It was like we were all thinking the same things and wrestling with our own minds to make sense of a situation that was so far removed from anything that we had experienced before. I have been to a lot of fatalities during the course of my duties and I have been to a major train crash before. But I was still shocked by what I saw and to this day I struggle fully to comprehend what it was that I was seeing.

If it was possible, the heat and the smoke seemed more intense inside; I could feel it around my body, almost as if it were putting physical pressure on me. There was a liquid on the walls of the tunnel and all over the walls and the floor of the train. I thought at first that this was some kind of condensation caused by the heat, but when I looked closer I realised that it was blood. It was everywhere and for the first time I noticed that I was standing in it. It was thick and slippery and when I looked down I could see the imprints that my boots had left in it.

I started to take my in surroundings in more detail. I found myself looking at objects and taking a while to work out what they were. They looked so out of place and unnatural, so far removed from what they should have looked like, that it took a second for me to realise that I was looking at the bodies of the people who had been on that train when the explosion happened. Bodies were piled on top of other bodies – the train had been packed and they had fallen on to each other. I think that all of the bodies I saw in that carriage were incomplete. All had either lost a limb or were completely disrupted by the blast. Nothing was moving; everything was deathly quiet. I thought that no one was left alive.

Then we were moving again, the paramedics were assessing each casualty as they moved deeper inside the train and prioritising them as they went. They had labels with the number priority marked on them so that they could be easily seen – priority one being the highest. More officers were entering the carriage behind me and I stopped and stood in the space for the first set of doors. I could see Glen and Gary now, they had entered just after me. They looked like ghosts in the gloom. There were no more that seven of us at that point because there simply was not room for anyone else. We had to wait for a bit then – we are reliant on the paramedics to tell us what to do and who to take out first. They are the ones with the experience and skill in this area, we are just the muscle.

I was still looking around trying to understand what I was seeing, and then I noticed that directly beside me, by the opposite set of doors, was a body. I found myself staring at it, unable to work out what was wrong. The man was obviously dead, but still I stared and stared; the sight was becoming nearly normal in that world so removed from our own. And then it hit me: the man was naked. I could see that all his clothes had been blown off him by the blast and he was lying there in the nude. I cannot explain why, but this surreal sight snapped me into action. I could not just stand there looking at the carnage inside that carriage, I would end up sending myself mad. I needed something to do, and quickly.

Chapter Six

THE CASUALTIES

There was the body of a woman lying at my feet; I had accepted her as part of my environment and was trying not to look at her. The paramedics had moved past her with only a cursory glance. I assumed that there was nothing that could be done for her and that she was dead. But then I looked down – and imagine my surprise when I saw that she was looking straight back. There was life in those eyes and she was trying to speak to me. She was a young woman with dark hair and from what I could see she was smartly dressed – it is difficult for me to describe individuals, though, because visibility was poor and everything was covered in dust and gore. I knelt down next to her and smoothed her hair off her face. She started to tell me the names of all the other people who were lying close to her on the train. This brave woman had been talking to all the other casualties, trying to keep them conscious despite her own injuries. I had partly resigned myself to the fact that we had been too late; it was only now that I even considered there might be people still alive here.

I was trying to reassure her and telling her that we would get her off at the earliest opportunity. I looked for the paramedics for advice, but they were busy trying to treat a woman with horrific injuries to her legs. I had to make the decision myself and the one I made was to get this woman out of this hell hole. I asked her if she had any injuries; I could not see any obvious ones, but there was nothing to say that damage hadn't been done internally. She told me that her back was hurting and that she hadn't moved because of this. I was reluctant to move her, but some of the questions that I had asked myself on the way down the tunnel were still unanswered and I did not know at this point if we had a limited amount of time.

We had no stretchers so I had no choice but to stand her up and move her off the carriage on foot so that she could be carried back to the station and safety. Another officer helped me get her onto her feet – I think it was Gary, but I really do not remember. She did not complain, but it was obvious that she was in a great deal of pain. I walked her slowly back down the carriage, stepping over various horrors as we went. I helped her down the steps and back into the tunnel, where I could see that more officers had arrived while I had been on the train. I left her being supported by a person on each side and went back on the train. I glanced over my shoulder as I was going through the carriage door only to see her now over the shoulder of a police officer I can only describe as a man mountain. He was running with her into the dark and carrying her as if she was a toy.

For the second time that morning, I entered the bomb-damaged carriage on the southbound Piccadilly Line. I was still aware that I needed to keep myself busy in order to keep my mind, so I started to check all of the bodies individually for signs of life that the paramedics had passed on their way up the train. I knew that the paramedics had chosen to leave the woman I had spoken to, presumably because she was not a priority, so what was to say that they hadn't done it to others as well? And what was stopping my colleagues and me getting them off while we were waiting for them to stabilise the more critically injured? Near the front of the train was a man lying on the floor between the two rows of seats. I must have stepped over him three times or more now, but it was the first time that I had noticed him. He was tall and slim, wearing a suit, I think – after all, this was a train full of commuters and everyone was going to work. I knelt down beside him and felt for a pulse in his neck; he was cold to the touch and his skin was dry, but I could feel a strong pulse beneath my fingers. He was unconscious, so I shook his shoulder in an attempt to bring him around. He groggily opened his eyes and looked at me; he tried to say something, but all that came out of his mouth was a croak. I leant in closer and eventually heard the word 'water'.

I was starting to think quite clearly by now, as if my mind had accepted the situation that I was in, and I was able to work without being distracted by the horror around me. I knew that most of the Underground drivers carried water with them when they were working. The Tube system is murderously hot in the summer, so I presumed that there would be water in the driver's cab. I stood up and took the few short steps into the cab and searched it for what I needed. It did not take long for me to locate a small hold-all on the floor underneath the driver's seat. I opened it and unceremoniously tipped the contents onto the floor. There was a crossword book in there, I think, and a light jacket, but there was also a small bottle of mineral water. I took this and returned to the side of the man I had just left. He had fallen out of consciousness again so I shook him awake and when he opened his eyes I showed him the water. He immediately opened his mouth and I poured a small amount in, just enough to wet his lips and the inside of his mouth. I could see that the inside of his mouth and his teeth were completely black where he had been inhaling that disgusting air for so long.

The water seemed to have brought him round a little and I started speaking to him. I asked him his name and asked if he was injured. I told him my name and that I was here to help him and get him off the train if he could manage to stand. He was whispering, so I could only just make out what he was saying, but he told me that he had an injury to his legs. We could have been the only people on the planet at this stage – I was so focused on what I was doing, I was not even considering my surroundings or anyone in them. The only thing that seemed real was me and the man on the floor in front of me. I had found a level that I could work at down there and it meant doing one thing at a time and concentrating only on that. If I had continued to take in my surroundings, I would have rendered myself useless and simply stood there in a daze.

I helped him to his feet and he shouted in pain, as his wounded legs protested at the fact that they were having to bear his weight. But as with the woman before, the only thing I could think to do was to get him off the train as quickly as I could. I took his weight, put his arm around my shoulder and led him to the exit. Again, when I looked down onto the tracks leading back to Russell Square I could see that more officers were arriving all the time. I helped the man down the metal steps and onto the tracks, where he was supported by the newly arrived officers who were waiting there to receive more of the injured. I would estimate that there were maybe fifteen officers down there on the tracks. They had formed a line, waiting to do their part in the evacuation; all looked nervous and in a little bit of shock. But I doubt that I looked any different, if not worse.

I shouted to an officer at the end of the line that we desperately needed stretchers and that he should go back to the surface then return with anything he could find that could be used to carry people. The officer did not even say a word to me – this was not a rank thing, this was about saving lives, and he simply turned around and ran back down the tunnel at full pelt.

This was now the third time that I had got back on that train, I did not want to be there, but I could not help but stay. It would have been easy to have gone back down the tunnel, assisting either the woman or the man, but I hadn't and I think I know the reason for this now. I had one last job to do that day – one that turned out to be the most important one of all for me.

Chapter Seven

MY GILL

I went back to my original position by the first set of doors in the carriage. I had run out of low-priority casualties to evacuate, so I had no choice but to wait for the paramedics to direct me further. The waiting around was making my time down there all the more difficult. Every time I stopped, I found myself taking in the scene and every time this happened, I noticed another atrocious sight. I thought that the best thing that I could do was just look at the floor by my feet. All over the floor of the carriage were the belongings of its occupants. There were handbags, wallets, mobile phones, several pairs of glasses, the floor was littered with it all. People's most important possessions strewn everywhere and forgotten in a life-changing instant.

I was still staring at the floor when one of the paramedics came to get me. He told me that they needed help moving the woman with the severe leg injuries, the one they had been working on when I was helping the injured man. I moved over to where she was and stood in the background while the woman paramedic explained what they planned to do to get her out. This was the first time I had had a chance to see the woman's injuries close up. She was on one of the bench seats on the left-hand side of the train about halfway down; she was sitting up and her back was leaning against the wall. Her legs were tucked up beneath her in a kind of foetal position. The right leg was completely gone. It looked like it had been skinned from the knee down and all the bone was exposed to the ankle joint. It did not seem real, it reminded me at the time of something you would see at a butcher's counter rather than attached to a person. The bone was so white; it looked like it had been cleaned. Her left leg was not much better; it was still attached, but was only so by the smallest amount of skin and muscle. It was bent away from her body at strange angle and I could tell that it could not be saved.

I am ashamed to say that I felt disgusted by these injuries; I did not want to go anywhere near them, the thought of touching them turned my stomach. I have experienced a lot of guilt since the event for having these feelings. I know that I was not in control of them at the time, but I could not help but feel bad for thinking of myself when there was someone who was obviously in great need of my help. It was only when someone said to me, just recently, that it doesn't matter what I felt – it was how I acted that mattered – that I have started to feel better about it. I suppose that, in respect of my actions, I didn't let my feelings interfere at all.

Someone had told me at one point that the woman we were preparing to help was called Gill. She was a young-looking woman with dark hair and a fair complexion. I would have said that she was in her early to mid-thirties, but it was hard to tell. She too had all the black stuff in her mouth; it really looked disturbing, like she had been drinking tar. I remember thinking that she might have been pretty under all that black soot. She was very pale and it was clear that she had lost a hell of a lot of blood. I could never have imagined at that point that this woman would have such a huge impact on my life in the future.

The paramedics had made a stretcher out of coats that they had gathered from the carriage. It was an ingenious bit of equipment and I remember thinking that they had done really well to improvise such a tool. The idea was to lay the stretcher in the walkway between the two seats and then lower the woman onto the coats so that she could be picked up and carried out. I ended up near her head and took hold of her left shoulder; on the word from the medic we lifted her up and put her into position on the makeshift stretcher. She did not make a sound through all of this, though I had expected her to feel a lot of pain because she was being lifted from a point quite near to her injuries by the people at her lower end.

Now we had to get her off the train and it would not be easy as there was only room in that confined space for one person at each end to carry the stretcher. I took the end near to her head and Gary took the end near her legs. We picked the stretcher up using the arms of the coats as handles and started to move towards the exit. It was hard going even at this early stage. I was walking backwards and kept slipping on the debris that covered the floor – both inanimate and human. As we got to the exit to the train, I shouted to the officers still waiting on the tracks to receive the wounded to help us, and standing at the bottom of the stairs was my mate Ray.

Ray is a wonderful character. He emigrated from Sierra Leone to England years ago. Ray is basically a gentle giant, a massive man with a heart of gold; he takes good care of his body and works out a couple of times a week. All that muscle on his six-foot-six frame makes for a very intimidating appearance, but Ray is as soft as shit when you get past his bulk. He is a very laid-back character and his work ethic differs somewhat from mine: where I run around like a headless chicken trying to do everything at the same time, Ray is a lot more particular about the work that he does and the jobs that the takes on. Despite our differences, Ray and I get on well; we have an understanding that suits both of us and we manage to co-exist. But he still won't give me an arm wrestle – I think I could take him with the wind behind me…!

Ray came to the base of the steps and I passed down the two coat arms that I was holding to him. As ingenious as the improvised stretcher was, it wasn't very stable and we had to be so careful that Gill didn't fall out. I then had to take the end that Gary had so that we could get the whole thing down onto the tracks. This was not as easy as it sounds: we were working in such a confined space that all the lifting was done at arm's length and as small as Gill was, it was still hard work. I took the end that Gary was holding, but because I was off balance I slipped on the blood that covered the floor. I really thought I was going to drop her, but somehow managed to wedge my body in the doorway to the train and stay on my feet. Once I stabilised myself, I lifted the stretcher past my body and faced the stairs again. I had to keep my arms very low, as Ray – who had the other end – was about three feet lower than I was. This, again, made things very difficult. I started to descend the steps, but as soon as I moved my feet I slipped on the blood again and I nearly ended up sitting in it.

How I managed to keep hold of Gill, I will never know. The makeshift handles on the stretcher were soaked in her blood and I had to wrap them around my fists just to keep my grip. I was scared to move; I knew we needed to get her out as quickly as possible, but if we had have dropped her, it might well have killed her. I had stood there for a couple of seconds, thinking my options through, when I felt someone grab the back of my belt. It was Gary. He told me to keep going, and that he would stop me from falling over forwards. Very gingerly, I started to climb down, putting all my trust in Gary not to let go. The steps are made of aluminium, I think; they have raised grips to stop you slipping, but with all the blood on them it was like walking on ice. The handrail was useless to me because my hands were full, but it was keeping Gary on his feet and he was holding us all together. Eventually, after a few scary moments and near misses, I made it onto the tunnel floor. The feeling of relief was profound but we still had a long way to go to get her out, I estimated our walk up the tunnel to be at least three-quarters of a mile.

People started to gather around Gill and me, eager to help, and we started to organise ourselves for the walk back to the Tube station. I looked back towards the train just in time to see Gary disappear back inside – he just would not leave.

The stretcher party consisted of four people: I was at the front on the left, Ray was behind me, the Railtrack guy was on the right of me and a Metropolitan Police officer was behind him on the right. We all got the best hold on the stretcher that we could and started down the tunnel into the gloom. It was hard going with the heat and the smoke, but my body had adjusted to it by this point and I didn't even consider it at the time. We were all treading on each other's feet as we were so close together and keeping hold of the coat sleeves was very hard – they were waterproof jackets, so they became very slippery with all the blood and sweat. By this point, I had gone onto a kind of autopilot; I do not think that I have ever been so focused on anything in my entire life. Everything was so simple: the only thing that I had to do was get this woman out of that tunnel and to somebody who could help her. I felt strong, like I could go on forever; I was not even breathing hard. The only way I could tell that my body was working hard was the amount of sweat that was drenching my body.

Surprisingly, Gill had remained conscious – her eyes were open and she was staring at the roof of the tunnel. We were all shouting encouragement at her and I was holding her hand with my free one, squeezing it every now and again when she started to close her eyes. I wanted this woman to live more than I have ever wanted anything in my life. I cannot explain the connection that I felt with her down there in the dark, but it was so strong that it was like I was willing her to stay alive and she could feel it.

I realise how this all sounds. I'm a bit of a realist and if I had heard this kind of account before my experiences that day I would have dismissed it as overdramatic 'crystal-hugging hippy shit'. But I felt it so strongly that it was almost physical and there is no explaining it.

I'm not sure how long we were going for before people started to complain that they were getting tired. There was no sense of time or distance in that tunnel; we could have been on another planet for all the difference that it made. I kept urging them to go on, but it made no difference. I was running on pure adrenaline and had been down there for a long time; I guess that the others did not have the benefit of that. I'm not criticising them at all, but like I said, I was functioning on a whole different level and felt like I could go on forever. We stopped and lowered Gill gently to the floor. It was then that I realised that my fingers on my right hand had gone blue and my hand was completely numb. We took a couple of seconds to sort ourselves out and did a straight swap with the person next to us. I was now on Gill's right-hand side and when we picked her up I held her hand again. We started to walk, but we had not gone far before she completely lost consciousness. We were shouting at her, trying to wake her, and I was squeezing her hand but she would not come round. I thought she had died on us. We stopped again and put the stretcher down. I tried to find the pulse in her neck but could find nothing. She was as cold as ice and her skin felt like rubber under my fingers. All of us were standing around her and I don't know about the others but I felt helpless. I was still looking for a pulse, but for the life of me I couldn't find one no matter where I looked; she did not even seem to be breathing. But just as I was about to give up she swallowed hard, her eyes opened and she looked at me. The relief was nearly overwhelming; I could not help but smile and squeeze her hand.

We started off again and tried to set a quicker pace. It was clear that Gill was running out of time; everyone of us knew the urgency of the situation. She lost consciousness at least twice more in that tunnel. Each time we would stop and go through the same routine as the first time, and each time she opened her eyes the relief was the same. I still cannot understand how she stayed alive. It had been at least an hour since the explosion, if not more, and still she was hanging on. She had lost so much blood that her wounds had stopped bleeding and the fact that I could not find a pulse or see the rise and fall of her chest was telling me that this woman was almost dead. I wanted to go faster but it was impossible. We were making the best progress that we could, but it seemed like everything was against us. Then, when I thought that nothing more could go wrong and the situation could not get any worse, the stretcher broke.

The coats had come untied in the middle somehow and we were forced to stop. None of us had actually seen the paramedics construct the stretcher, so we had no way of knowing how to put it back together. We were at a complete loss and I was losing patience with the situation. We must have stood there for a couple of precious minutes discussing what we could do. It was not like we could just pick her up by her arms and legs because of her injuries and no matter how hard we tried we could not reconstruct the stretcher. In the end I turned to Ray and said to him, 'Fuck it, put her on my shoulder.' Ray and one of the others picked her up and put her on my left shoulder with her head and arms over my back and her legs on my chest just underneath my chin. She screamed – I can still hear it now as I am writing. She had hardly made a sound before this and now she was screaming in agony every time I took a step. We could not have known it at the time, but Gill's legs were not her only injury. During the explosion, she had taken some shrapnel in her back.

She was obviously in a great deal of pain, but I could not stop; I had no other option other than to carry on. For the first time I found the going hard. I was now soaked with blood as well as sweat and Gill was slipping off my shoulder. I had wrapped my arm as tightly as I could around her waist, but the harder I gripped the more she was crying out. Ray was walking beside me and trying to push her back onto my shoulder, but we were fighting a losing battle. Before, I had felt that I could go on forever; now I was starting to get tired. My legs felt like lead, I was breathing so hard that my chest was burning and I could taste blood in my mouth. The lactic acid was building up in my shoulder and that also felt like it was on fire. Gill was still screaming with the pain of it. I couldn't go on. I had no option but to stop again and I was furious with myself.

I lowered her to the floor, with Ray's help, and again we

started to discuss our options. One of the guys had had the foresight to bring the coats and we started to put the stretcher together as best as we could. We managed to put it back almost as it was, but it did not look very sturdy. It was placed between the rails and we lifted Gill on to it. Once more we picked her up and started walking, but we had only gone a small distance when it broke again and she nearly fell through it. I was nearly crying with frustration. It seemed like nothing we did worked, all we could do was look at each other and try to think of some other option. We still did not know how far we had come or how far we had to go; as I have already said, we had no sense of time or distance. I was just about to try and pick her up again when an officer appeared in the tunnel in front of us carrying an arm full of blankets. It was the same officer that I had asked to go back down the tunnel earlier and he had come back with exactly what we needed. The relief that swept over me was indescribable. We still had a chance to save the life of this woman; we might still have time to get her out of this nightmare.

The blanket was laid out on the floor and we lifted Gill onto it, took up our former positions and set off once again. The going was easy now compared to what it had been, we were making good progress and were nearly jogging. It only took a couple of minutes before we saw the end of the tunnel and the light of the platform.

I was ecstatic and angry all at the same time. We had made it, but we only had a couple of hundred yards to go when I had given up carrying her. I could have made that distance if I had tried a little harder, I am sure of it. If this woman died because of the time that I had wasted, I would never forgive myself. There were officers waiting at the edge of the platform and we passed Gill up to them. We then all climbed up, reassumed our previous positions around the blanket and picked her up again. None of us was leaving her at this stage after coming so far.

Someone had told us that the lifts were working again and that we could use them to take her to the booking hall and help. This was really good news, because I do not think that I had the strength left at this stage to take her up the stairs. We got in a lift and laid her on the floor. She was still conscious, but when I held her hand and squeezed it there was no response. Someone handed me a bottle of water and I poured a little onto her lips. Then someone took it off me from behind and poured the entire contents over her face. I'm not sure who this was, but it pissed me off for some reason — I can't explain why.

Also in the lift was the woman that I had found on the floor of the train. She looked terrible in the light. She was cowering in the corner of the lift and was looking at us and Gill with the most pitiful look in her eyes that I have ever seen. Seeing her in the lift gave me a little perspective on the time we had taken to get from the train to the station and accomplish everything that had been done before and during that time. It really couldn't have taken that long if we had caught up with her, and this made me feel a little better. Time had stood still in that tunnel. What had probably only taken an hour had seemed like it had lasted a day.

We reached ground level and carried Gill into the

booking hall. The scene that greeted us there was pure chaos. There were so many people there, all injured and being treated or helping out in some way. There were doctors, nurses, paramedics, police officers, station staff and people off the street that had come to help out. We took Gill into the booking hall and laid her on the floor next to the ticket barriers. I got the attention of a paramedic and started to explain Gill's injuries to him. The bloke was just staring at me blankly; I had to shout at him to get his attention properly. It wasn't until later, when I looked in the mirror, that I realised he was probably shocked by our appearances more than anything else. Satisfied that I had given him all the information that I could, and that Gill was going to get treated, I turned back towards the lifts and prepared myself to go back underground.

Chapter Eight

NOBODY LEFT

I walked back round to the lifts and met up with everyone there. They had found some water and were all drinking greedily. I took a bottle for myself and downed the whole thing in one go. I did not realise until then how dehydrated I actually was. After I had finished that bottle I grabbed another and started to drink at a more normal pace. Ray was busy stripping off his kit. He had been wearing his full operational equipment throughout the whole of Gill's rescue. If I had been him I would have dumped it in the tunnel a long time ago.

We were all standing outside the lifts, waiting for one to arrive; we weren't really talking all that much, but there was a great deal for us all to think about. There was a strange feeling of normality about standing there waiting for the lift – it is one of those day-to-day things we do that you never really think about. The only reason that I think that it stuck out in my mind this time is because it was about the first normal thing that I had done since receiving that first call. I stood there for a while in a bit of a daze before I snapped out of it. There were still people on that train and we needed to get back down there.

We all made our way back down onto the platform via the stairs. About halfway down we heard an explosion. From our position on the stairs it sounded like a rumble far off in the distance and we all thought that a secondary device had gone off in the tunnel. Little did we know at that point that a bus had exploded in Tavistock Square a few roads away and more people had lost their lives on this dreadful day.

This is where the next bit gets confusing for me. I can remember being eager to get back to the train and I can remember picking up an armful of blankets that were lying about on the platform, but that's about it. Ray told me later that I left them and ran back down the tunnel, but I can't really confirm or deny that. I remember being back in the tunnel briefly, because I passed John with two officers still walking down the tunnel. We must also have overtaken them when we were carrying Gill, but I did not notice as I was so focused on the job in hand.

The next thing that I remember is being back at the train. I was on my own, all the officers that were standing outside were gone, and there was the body of a woman on the floor of the tunnel at the bottom of the steps. She was covered with a blanket and had one of the medics' tags on her. It was black with the word 'DEAD' written on it in white. I remembered her from the train – she had been on the bench seat opposite Gill. Gary told me later that she had died really suddenly. One minute she was talking normally, the next she was gone and despite the paramedics' best efforts she could not be revived.

I stepped around the body of the woman and walked up the steps of the train for what was to be the last time. The scene had changed a little from the time that I had left with Gill. The emergency services from the King's Cross end had made it to the bomb-damaged train and there were fire brigade and a doctor in the carriage. Gary and the Governor were still there and there were about another five officers with them. Everyone seemed to be standing around and waiting; I guessed from this that there was no one left to be saved. We were all feeling spaced out and I started talking to Gary about my journey down the tunnel with Gill and what it was like upstairs. We stood there and chatted for a while, waiting for something more to do, but I had a suspicion that we would be leaving very soon.

About ten minutes passed. Ray and the others had just got back to the train, and Gary and I were still waiting inside the carriage. I was watching the medics, fire brigade and the doctor checking and re-checking all the bodies in the carriage for signs of life. It was a difficult scene to watch. I knew that there was no one left, as I had been on the train since the beginning and I could account in my head for those that we had initially found alive. All of them had been evacuated. It wasn't long before the doctor called a halt to the search and confirmed what I already knew. He said that we had done all we could and that there were no more survivors; for our own safety, we had to leave. Even though I knew this was coming, I didn't want to believe it and I didn't want to go. I did not want to accept that we had to leave so many people in that train and that so many were dead. The Governor started to organise our exit from the scene; we all filed out of the front of the train through the driver's cab, down the metal steps, around the body of the woman covered by the blanket and onto the tracks. I didn't even look back. I had seen enough for one day.

All the paramedics' kit was lying on the floor of the tunnel, so we divided it up between us and started to walk back down the tunnel. I was walking with Gary and Ray, and I think my friend Chris was there at this point as well. Anyway, I think we had all started to go into shock at this point – it was like we were walking in the park on the way back down that tunnel. Gary and I were laughing and joking, I was taking the piss out of him for keeping his tie and stab vest on through the whole incident and Gary was taking it out of me for being a scruffy bastard. Gary looked at all the blood and grime on my shirt and commented that it looked cleaner than it did on a normal working day. He said that instead of blood and soot, my shirt was normally covered in tomato sauce and coffee stains. It seemed really weird that we were acting like this at the time, but I realise now that our minds were trying to shut out the experience that we had just been through.

I know that there were other officers there on that day that I haven't mentioned, because I have seen them since and spoken to them about what they did. But the simple fact of the matter is that I can't remember them being there. As I have already said, I was focusing so intently on what I was doing that I didn't have to take in my surroundings and I must have missed people along the way. There were a lot of things that happened on that train that I was not involved in, but again I can't tell you about those either for the same reason. I took enough of that day away with me to last a lifetime of bad memories and I'm glad I can't remember every detail of every event.

The walk back took about ten or fifteen minutes. I had more time on the return trip to take in my surroundings and could see evidence of the rescue everywhere. There were discarded pieces of medical equipment and supplies, blankets and empty water bottles and bits of police equipment that had been dropped all along the length of the tunnel. Someone had also been along the tunnel and deposited full bottles of water every fifty metres or so. I had missed these on my way to the train the last time, but I certainly drank my fill on the way back. We arrived back at the platform and went directly to the lifts. No one was saying much any more; all of us were lost in our own thoughts about the events of that morning. Gary and I stuck together – we had attached ourselves to the paramedics as we were still carrying their kit. The five of us got in the next lift and went up to the booking hall, walked through the chaos up there and directly out of the front of the station. No one even glanced at us; it was like we didn't exist. The road was packed solid with emergency vehicles and we slipped through them and across the road to Tesco. I looked at my watch for the first time now. It was midday. I was surprised that only a relatively short period had passed. I had half expected it to be dark when I left the Tube station.

Chapter Nine

A STATE
OF SHOCK

The staff in Tesco were great – they said we could take anything in the store that we needed, but all I wanted was more water and a cigarette. I reached into my pockets for my death sticks but all I pulled out was a pulpy mess that used to be a packet of twenty. Gary and I were shown out the back to the delivery entrance; we sat on some pallets and smoked Gary's cigarettes in silence for a while. We briefly talked about the things that we had done and Gary told me about how the blanket-covered woman had died on him when he and others were trying to get her off the train. He seemed upset about this more than other events of the day. I could relate to him in this respect, as I had connected with one of the casualties that day and I found myself wondering about her fate.

We went back into the store after what must have been ten

minutes, or three cigarettes each. We had both been trying to use our mobile phones for a while now, but neither of us could get a reception. Unbeknown to us, the mobile-phone network in London had been suspended so that no more devices could be activated remotely. We approached a member of staff in the store and asked if we could use his landline. We needed to call home – my mum and Gary's wife would probably be beside themselves. We had to wait for a while in line behind the medics, but when my time came, I dialled the number of my mum's pub. She picked up the phone and sounded stressed before even I said it was me. All I said to her was that I had been heavily involved in the events of the day but that I was OK and that I would be home at some point. With this I hung up to let someone else have their turn.

I spent the next few minutes hanging around in the shop. I acquired myself some more cigarettes, smoked a little more out the back with Gaz and drank as much water as I could. I felt very light-headed because I was so dehydrated after all that time working in the intense heat of the tunnel; if I hadn't drunk that water, I would have passed out for sure. But even after all I had been through that day I still couldn't settle, I still wanted to do more. I stood up, left Gary where he was staring into space and walked out the front of the shop into the street. I walked around looking for someone who looked like they were in charge.

Standing just outside the Tube station, surrounded by other police officers, was a senior officer that I knew well. He used to work at my police station before he got promoted and I knew him as a decent and approachable officer with a very down-to-earth view. I made my way over to him through the crowd and waited beside him until he had finished talking. He was the senior police officer on the scene and if anybody needed something done it would be him. While I was waiting, I noticed all the police that were standing around doing nothing. I suspect now that they had been placed in reserve in case of something else happening, but at the time it infuriated me. There had been so few of us at the Russell Square end of the train, we could have used more. He finished talking and turned to me. 'Is there anything you need me to do, Guv?' I asked him. He just stood there looking at me for a second then turned to a group of officers standing around near their vehicle a few yards away and said, 'Somebody come and take care of this man!' I was shocked, all I wanted was to help and I was being dismissed. I still felt a bit spaced-out and couldn't make sense of the situation. Not until a short time later would it all fall into place. One of the officers came and over to me and put his hand gently on my arm, but I was still looking at the chief inspector. He had real pity in his eyes and I could not understand why. Then, in a voice that you would use when talking to a child who had scraped his knee, he said to me, 'We are centralising the casualties in a hotel around the corner, I want you to go there.' I was led off by the officer.

We got a few yards up the road and then I remembered Gary. 'My mate Gaz is still in Tesco, we need him with us,' I told the officer, and I went to look for my friend. The officer followed me back into the store and I found my mate still inside with the medics. They were just standing around staring into space, a state that was slowly becoming the norm. I told them that we were being moved and they all followed the officer and me to the Holiday Inn around the corner, which was being used as the casualty collection point.

We entered the hotel through the service entrance in the back and walked into one of the conference rooms. There were a lot of people about inside the hotel, a few of them had injuries but no one at this point was serious. I guessed that all the seriously injured had been evacuated by this time – after all, it was over three hours since the attack had happened. We milled around for a while, drinking tea and talking among ourselves. It was hard not to be doing anything after all the non-stop activity that morning, though, and I just couldn't settle. More and more officers and emergency-service personnel were arriving at the hotel and all had that far-away look in their eyes; like us, they milled around doing a lot of nothing and talking quietly. It was strange to be surrounded by the relatively clean surroundings of the hotel after spending so long underground. None of us looked like we should be there; we looked like we belonged on a battlefield. Or, at least, that's the way they looked to me – I still did not have a clue what I looked like.

I must have made my way to the toilet half an hour after arriving at the hotel. I had taken on a lot of liquid and suddenly badly needed to go to the loo. I followed the directional signs into the lobby, then to the Gents and the first thing I did when I got inside was to look in the mirror. I froze. I did not recognise the man looking back at me. It was like I had been numb before but the sight of me brought all the feeling back into my body. I looked like a cross between a chimney sweep and a butcher, altogether nothing like a police officer. My hair looked like straw, it was all matted together with dirt, and I dread to think what else. My face was black but was streaked where I had been sweating and the clean lines broke up the black. I was horrified to see that the inside of my mouth was black, just like the casualties on the train. It looked like I had eaten a blackjack, like you used to get in a mixed bag of penny sweets when you were a kid. And the taste was foul, it was the smell of burning hair from the tunnel. I vomited in the sink instantly.

I had come to work that morning in a clean pressed shirt and despite what Gary would have you believe I'm normally quite smartly turned out. But now my shirt was just a rag. I had lost the first four buttons somehow and it was opened to below my chest. It was no longer white, it was covered in blood, but where I had sweated so much it had turned an orangey yellow colour. My trousers were filthy as well. Even though they were black, you could see the dirt on them, but it was not just dirt, it was blood as well. The fronts of my thighs were shining with the stuff and when I rubbed my hands down them they came away pink. There was also blood on my boots and I do not even want to talk about what I saw when I looked at the soles – you can use your own imagination for that. I was starting to cool down now, my body temperature must have been through the roof with all the heat that I had been exposed to, and towards the end of the rescue I had stopped sweating as though I had symptoms of heat stroke. But my clothes were still drenched; they felt like I had jumped into the sea with them on. Every part of me was soaked and every time I took a step my boots squelched with all the moisture inside. I spent a good deal of time in that bathroom trying to put in to perspective the events of the day and being sick on an empty stomach. I understood now why the CI had looked at me so pitifully. I was a wreck.

The next couple of hours passed without incident. We hung around the hotel drinking coffee and smoking a disgusting amount. Glen came and joined Gary, Ray, Chris and me and he had a good number of our cigarettes – even though we found out later that he had his own. Everyone we encountered who had not been involved in the rescue looked at us the same way that the CI had. It began to infuriate me: why should we be pitied when so many people had lost their lives and were still on that train where we had left them?

A woman that I knew from work turned up and stood with us outside while we were smoking ourselves into an early grave. She was in a real state. That morning she had been on her way to our old force headquarters in Tavistock Place. From what she was saying, she had been only a short distance from the bus when it had exploded and had been one of the first on scene. Emotionally she was in bits, but none of us knew what to say to her. All of us were still in shock and feeling numb, and as much as I wanted to empathise with her, I couldn't. All I could do in the end was put my arm around her and give her a cigarette – after all, that was all we were doing.

By now, I was getting bored with hanging around. I was trying to avoid thinking and all the sitting about was not helping me achieve that. I started to wander around the hotel and look for something to take my mind off things. I strolled into the bar and was greeted by the same pitiful look from the staff and the customers, but I ignored them as the television was on. Sky News was on a fifty-inch flat screen and for the first time that day I realised how big a deal this was. The headline read something like SUICIDE BOMBS. This was the first time that I considered this possibility, even after all I had seen. I knew that we had been attacked, but I hadn't even thought about how that attack had been implemented. I am ashamed to say that the first thought that went through my mind after receiving this information was, 'I hope I trod on the bastard'. The four bombs that had brought London to a standstill were the sole topic of the broadcast. The newsreader seemed to know more than I did, and I had been there – that was a weird feeling, I can tell you. I watched that TV for about an hour, rooted to the spot. I could not believe that something like this had happened in my country, let alone where I work. The extent of the attack was staggering: three simultaneous explosions on the Tube system and one later on a bus. God only knew at this point how many people had lost their lives. I had estimated then that we left thirty bodies on the train at Russell Square and as it turned out I wasn't that far from the mark. Also, at the back of my mind I knew that I had friends at each of the scenes. Most of my team was at Russell Square by now, but a few of them were missing. My thoughts went out to them and I hoped that they had not experienced what we had, though I knew that was unlikely.

After getting as much information as I could from the TV, I went back to join up with the others. There was now an officer standing around with them, but he was remarkably clean. He came up to me as I approached and told me simply, 'That woman Gill has died.' I felt an instant rage rise up inside of me that it took every ounce of strength I had left to contain. How could she be dead? She was alive when I left her. How did this officer know? I didn't want to believe it. I have already said how personal an experience Gill's rescue was for me; I put everything I had into it. It had left me exhausted, mentally and physically. But at least I had thought that she had survived it and that justified everything that I and the others with me had done. I instantly went to pieces. Everything that I had done or failed to do in that tunnel came back to me in an instant. I blamed myself for her death and that was all there was to it. I went back into the bathroom and vomited some more. Afterwards, I sat on the toilet and for the first time that day I cried.

I am conscious about sounding full of self-pity at this stage of my account. I was all over the place. I did not know what to think or what to feel. How was I supposed to act? Was I supposed to suck it up and show some backbone? That's what I felt like I was supposed to do at the time. Even up until now my experiences in that train have been a very private thing for me. I have never spoken about it to anyone in any kind of detail. The people closest to me know that I was there and they kind of know what I did, but I have never spoken about what I was feeling at the time, or what I had seen, to anyone. Even at the time of writing this account, 15 months later, I have not. I have had therapy, but still I have only been made to think about the event and not talk about it. In the year since the attacks on London, I have gone through a personal hell and it nearly drove me mad. It is only now that I have started to come out of the other side of it that I feel strong enough to write this. But I still have to stop every now and again because I get too upset to continue writing. So please bear with me, I can only tell you what I felt at the time.

After I pulled myself together again, I left the bathroom and went back to the others. Things seemed to be happening now, as rumours were flying around about what was going to happen with us. Some people were saying we were to be redeployed around London to help out at the other scenes, but I thought that unlikely, given the state we were in. I had lost most of my kit and I have already mentioned what we looked like. The most realistic theory was that we were to be moved to Holborn Police Station, where we would be debriefed by the anti-terrorism officers, but no matter who we asked we could not get this confirmed. All I wanted to do by now was go home and get clean, I didn't care about anything else. I was getting pissed off – we all were. We had been waiting in that hotel for over four hours now with only our memories of the day to occupy our minds.

A short time later, Glen came to see us. He had been flitting about all afternoon trying to keep in the loop so that he could look after us and to give us information. He told us that we were indeed to go to Holborn to be debriefed. It felt good to know what we were doing, at least. The plan was that we were going to walk there, as it was only a short distance away. We gathered ourselves up and started to get organised. I still had the van outside, so I asked if anyone wanted a lift and those that did jumped in with me. I really shouldn't have been driving, but no one stopped me and I didn't really think about it until afterwards. My female colleague, Chris and another officer – I can't remember exactly who it was – came in with me and we slowly drove out of the scene, navigating around all the vehicles that were still outside the station. We left the inner cordon and went out onto the main road that leads towards Holborn Tube. The outer cordon was halfway down this road and it was manned by the Met. They lifted the police tape up for us and we drove away from the scene more than seven hours after we had arrived.

Chapter Ten

FRUSTRATION

It was only when we were driving to the police station that the jarring normality of the city struck me. Apart from the fact that there were more pedestrians about than usual, you would not have believed that London had suffered its worst attack since the Blitz. Shops were open; people in suits were walking on the pavements carrying their briefcases as if nothing had happened. I was angry. How could these people act normally after all this had happened? Why were the streets not as deserted as they were inside the cordon? Apart from the TV crews dotted about, it could have been a normal day in town.

I drove on to my destination through the rush-hour traffic, pulling up to the police station a short time later. The others that had walked had arrived before us and were all waiting outside. Some nutter on a pushbike wearing a German army helmet with a picture of Saddam Hussein on it had been harassing them on their walk round. Big mistake – he got nicked. He was in cuffs when I got out of the van and went to wait with the others. I don't think he had realised what he had done until that point, or what the officers around him had been through. But when I was told what he had been doing, I gave him a look you wouldn't believe and he shied away from me instantly. He knew then.

We waited in the street, still wondering what was to be done with us. People started to come up to us and ask us questions. We barely resembled police officers at this stage; we looked like shit. But still people were still coming up to us and asking directions, train times, what was open, was the Tube running, all sorts of random stuff. But that's not the worst thing. When we could not answer, some of them even had the nerve to get annoyed. I couldn't believe it. We looked like we had been blown up ourselves, but we were still expected to answer their questions. Gaz and I went and sat in the van, closed the doors and ignored the world. I understand now that these people were confused and probably scared – their first instinct would be to ask a police officer – but at the time I couldn't care less.

Glen had disappeared on us again; when he came back he looked angry. He had been inside the station and had found out that we were to be moved again. This was getting stupid; all of us had just had enough. But we were being herded around like cattle. This time we were to go to a hotel down the road to get debriefed and have what was left of our uniform seized as evidence. 'OK, let's go,' I thought. This time I piled as many officers in the van as I could and drove two minutes down the road to the hotel. The mood had gone from one of sorrow to one of anger since leaving the Holiday Inn. We were all very raw and very tired and all this messing about was doing none of us any good.

The next hotel was a posh one. I would have felt out of place there even if I had been dressed up; now I looked like Bruce Willis after going through all of the *Die Hard* films back to back. We were ushered into a massive conference room with scores of other officers from all over London and finally got a decent brief on what was to be done with us. There were piles of new uniforms on the floor and we were told to find our sizes and take what we needed. It was all jumbled up and there were no boots but in the end I ended up with a new shirt and trousers. We were then directed to go to a certain room in the hotel, where our old clothing would be taken from us for evidential use. We all followed the instructions given, but the hotel was huge and we got lost. Nothing was going right this day. Eventually, we found the room and went in one by one to see the anti-terrorism officers and give them our uniforms. There was no privacy – we stripped in front of everyone and put the uniforms into brown paper bags. I kept my boots.

This took a while, but I was one of the first in, so I waited for Gaz and then we both went back downstairs and waited in the conference room. More waiting around ensued and more smoking and coffee drinking went with it. This whole thing had been organised by the Metropolitan Police – we had still heard nothing from our own force. We all felt like we had done our bit for the day and just wanted to go home. It was about six o'clock now and we were still hanging around. Nothing was in place to deal with us and we were suffering because of it. We had all been at work for 12 hours or more and really did not need to be there. Not knowing what we were supposed to be doing, and not knowing where we were going, was making things worse for us. We all had to get home – I needed to get away from London.

We hung around for a while longer before we were told that we had to move again. We were told to go to King's Cross to meet with a team of medical staff that our occupational health team had set up. Off we went. I packed as many in the van as I could, but most had to walk as there were about a dozen of us by now.

I hadn't gone far when the plan changed once more. Because of the scene at King's Cross, the occupational health lot couldn't get to the offices through the cordon. We were redirected to our force headquarters in Tavistock Place. This presented its own problems, as I could not get there because of all the cordons around the bus. The day really was as frustrating as it sounds. In the end, I just drove through a load of no entry signs and ended up there more by luck than judgment. We were directed to some more offices, where we waited around. A woman came to see us, briefly chatted to us and gave us some drinks – but that was it. In the end, the Governor put his foot down. He told the staff at HQ that we were leaving and despite their protests we were off. I drove back to the station and dumped the van outside, grabbed all my kit from inside and stormed into the station. I threw my stuff in my locker and went to sit in the canteen. I was livid. I had been through hell and back, I should have been sent home hours ago. But, instead, I had been messed around for nearly eight hours after the event and still we had achieved nothing apart from getting a change of clothing and smoking ourselves half to death.

The Governor disappeared again to go and talk to the powers that be, but when he returned he told us that we had been released to go home. This was just in time, because I was just about to leave anyway. I grabbed a lift to Victoria from an officer who was hanging about and just managed to get the nine o'clock train home. Thank God, the mainline trains were running again, I couldn't have spent another minute in town.

Chapter Eleven

ISOLATION

I sat right at the back of the train and stared into space for an hour and twenty-five minutes on the way home. I can't even remember what I was thinking about, if I was thinking about anything at all. I arrived home just before eleven at night. I was living on my own at this point in my life and didn't fancy the prospect of going back to an empty house. I got a taxi from the station to my mum's pub and walked into what is effectively my second home.

Given the time of night it was I could have told you who would be in there and where they would be sitting before I even walked in the door. It is that kind of pub. It has a good base of regulars as well as a passing trade, as it is on a main road. I walked in the door and my mum came up to me straight away and hugged me. I could tell from that instant that she had been drinking a lot. After the ordeal that I had been through that day, this pissed me off. All I wanted was some normality and it was clear that I was not going to get any. I sat at the bar next to one of the regulars and was handed a cup of tea by someone. I wasn't saying much, I was just staring into my drink and everyone was leaving me alone; I do not think that they quite knew what to say to me. I'm not sure how much time passed, but when I went to take the first sip of my tea, it was stone cold.

I made idle chatter to the regulars for a while but avoided talking about my day. It was a strange experience to be immersed in this normal world. I smoked constantly but avoided having a real drink. I couldn't let myself get drunk – I would have gone to pieces.

I ran out of cigarettes fairly soon, but I had an unopened packet that I had bought on the way home. I put my hand in my pocket to get them but one of my epaulettes that I had been wearing all day came out as well. I had taken these off at the hotel in Holborn when my shirt was taken from me. I looked at these for a moment and what I saw made me break down. The numbers on our epaulettes are metal pin badges that are raised just above the material and caught up in them was a clump of Gill's hair.

The sight of this brought everything back in an instant. The tunnel, the train, the bodies, the blood, Gill's rescue attempt and the fact that she had died despite all our efforts. I was in bits. I do not cry in public, so I ran into the kitchen and ended up on my knees crying until it hurt my chest. Nobody came in after me.

I only cried for a minute at the most. I forced myself to

pull it together; I needed to get a grip on myself. People could not see me like this. I splashed my face with cold water and as I did this I noticed the state of my hands. I hadn't thought to wash them at any point during the day and they were black. Under my nails was the worst; God knows what I had been putting my hands in throughout the day. So I stood at the basin and scrubbed them clean. It was at this point that my mum came in. She was still very drunk and started to make a fuss of me, in that really over-the-top way that inebriated people do. I couldn't handle this any more, I couldn't go home and be on my own, but I didn't want to be surrounded by these drunken people either. So I took myself upstairs into my mum's flat and sat in front of the TV – not really watching it, but at least it stopped me thinking too much.

I heard my mum close the pub and she and her boyfriend of the time came upstairs. I was in the kitchen at this stage, drinking a cup of tea. They came in and tried to talk to me, but I wasn't being very receptive. My opinion at the time was that they were both drunk and there was no point in telling them anything, as they wouldn't remember anyway. I think now that I was just avoiding facing the issue, a trend that would last until the time I started writing this book.

It sounds like I am being really harsh about my mum writing this. The simple fact of the matter is that I love her very much, but we have never had a very emotionally close relationship and I have never been able to talk to her about my concerns or worries. We are alike in many ways and neither of us handles stressful situations very well.

I showered later that night. I had been longing to get clean all day but had forgotten about it by the time I arrived back home. I had popped home to get my uniform for the following day and had grabbed a change of clothes for that night. I only live a minute away from the pub, so I did not have to be on my own for long. As I was standing in the shower, I saw that the water had run black. The filth of that day was washing off me, out of my hair, off my skin, and I felt human for the first time since that morning. I stayed in there for about twenty minutes, just standing under the showerhead, cleansing my body. Then, for the first of many times in the days and weeks to follow, I coughed and what came out of my lungs was jet black.

I stayed up most of that night trying to sleep on the sofa in my mum's front room. I kept the TV on because I did not want to think or to be on my own in the dark. I knew that I had to get some sleep, because I was due back into work the next day and I did not have a clue what the day was to bring.

That night went on for what seemed to be a lifetime; my thoughts were of the events of that day no matter how I tried to block them out. Images of the horrors that I had seen would jump into my head and send me back into that train. I could feel the heat, smell that putrid smell and my breathing would quicken as though I were breathing in the smoke. I relived the whole incident again and again until I fell asleep out of exhaustion. Then I dreamed about it.

The next morning, my mum and her partner trod on eggshells around me. I was going through every emotion on the scale. One minute I would be morose, the next I would be like a bear with a sore head and sometimes I would even laugh. I didn't eat anything that morning. I hadn't eaten since dinner the night before last, but I had no appetite. I was fuming that I had to go to work that day after the events of the previous day, but at least I would be able to catch up with the guys I worked with and the other officers who had been at the other scenes in London.

Chapter Twelve

THE NEXT DAY

At about nine o'clock, I left for the train station and started the journey into work. Normally, I will sit on the train quite happily and read a book or listen to music and fall asleep. But not that day. I sat there and stared into space, thinking about everything and nothing all at the same time. The journey seemed to last an age. I was worried about what they would make me do at work and I was worried about the state in which I would find the city I love so much.

I arrived at London Victoria and was amazed to see that the Tube was open. The mainline station was not nearly as busy as it should have been, but then I guessed that all the sensible people had stayed at home that day. I walked down into the Tube station and it all came at me again.

I have never been so nervous in my life. I had not thought before that getting on the Tube would be such a big deal, but here I was 24 hours after being in the train at Russell Square and I was physically reliving my experience. It was the same thing that had happened to me the night before. It was like my body was preparing itself to go through the same experience again. I had consciously to take every step towards the Victoria Line and I kept saying to myself in my head, 'Get a grip, son, don't be a fucking spineless idiot.' In that way, I coached myself down the escalators and onto that northbound train.

Everybody in my carriage was nervous, you could feel the tension in the air. The Tube at this time of the day should have been busy. But there were no more than fifteen people in my carriage. Everybody was looking at one another suspiciously and I was getting my own fair share of dodgy looks. Only then did I realise that being dark-skinned and carrying an army-style rucksack, I looked like your average potential bomber. It made me feel bad that these people would think that of me, but they could have been forgiven taking into account the events of the previous 24 hours. The whole city was on edge.

The train sped to its destination and I found myself looking out of the window into the tunnel. I was watching the tunnel lights whizz past and suddenly I was back there again, standing outside the bomb-damaged train, looking at it silhouetted in the darkness. This was getting stupid. I couldn't keep my mind on where I was or what I was doing. How was I supposed to work today?

It is approximately nine minutes from Victoria Station to my destination, Warren Street, but even in that short amount of time I managed to relive the whole incident in my mind. When I got off the train at the platform I was a sweaty mess, breathing hard and wide-eyed. I walked as fast as I could to get out of that station. I just needed to be in the fresh air again. God only knows what I must have looked like to the other commuters. I ran more than walked out of the station and then it was over. I was in the open again and I slowly began to feel normal. I had got on a Tube train just over 24 hours after the events of the day before. It had not been pleasant in any sense of the word, but I was pretty sure I could do it again and that it would get easier every time.

I walked into work and was struck by how quiet it was. I expected it to be a hive of activity, but there were less people around than on a normal day. I was told later that there were more police officers on duty at that time than had ever been before in London. Officers had been called in from their homes and were working extraordinary hours just to keep pace with all the work that needed to be done.

As well as having to provide officers for our normal duties and commitments, the force had to provide officers to man all the cordons and start the investigation into the incident. This was only the beginning, as after the investigation was complete at the three sites that were under our jurisdiction, officers would have to go underground and recover the bodies and the property that had been left behind. I made a conscious decision at this point that I would have nothing to do with any of it. I couldn't even sit on a Tube train without cracking up; I could not expose myself to this incident any more.

I found the rest of the team in the canteen, drinking tea

and chatting among themselves. I sat down with them and asked them all how they were doing. Nothing specific, just general chit-chat as if it were a normal day. No one had told us what we were required to be in work for, so we had the same feelings of confusion and frustration that we had had the day before. We were all of the opinion that we could have all used at least one day at home to rest before being called into work, but we had resigned ourselves to the fact that this was not going to happen.

I spent most of the next hour or so with Gary and Chris, smoking outside the station. Gary was in a foul mood and was moaning about things more than usual. All this waiting around, both today and the day before, was driving us all mad. We had too much time to think, all of us were reliving the events of the previous day in our minds and we were all worried about what we were to be doing workwise. None of us wanted to go to any of the scenes because we didn't want to be exposed to that environment again. It would be too much too soon.

I was getting angry with the situation and the way we were being treated. The day before we had been herded around like cattle to no end, and today we had been called in from our homes just to be kept waiting around with no direction whatsoever. I am not normally an overtly angry man – I tend to suppress these feelings and remain calm on the outside. But today I could not. I was pacing up and down, swearing and cursing the administration; I was snapping at my colleagues and working myself up into a state of rage. I am not sure how much of this was evident to my friends around me, but I was not making much attempt to hide my feelings. The initial shock of the day before was wearing off, my emotions were starting to come through and the most prominent of these was anger.

I am not angry with my police force now and my feelings calmed down not long after the incident. At that time, though, I was only concerned with my own state of mind. I could feel myself slipping slowly into insanity and all I wanted to do was go home, relax and try to sort out in my mind what I had been through and figure out what long-term effects my experiences were going to have on me. I realise now that although my colleagues and I had played a large part in the events on the day before, we were now small parts in a very big machine and although we had to be considered, we had to wait our turn in the much bigger picture. My force has generally been good to me in the time since the bombings. The Occupational Health side of our organisation has been fantastic, but I am hoping some of the line managers will read this and that it will make them realise what effects such a traumatic event can have on an individual. At times – through no fault of their own – they have made me feel like I have been overreacting and milking the situation. This has put more pressure on me, which in turn has extended my recovery period, when all I wanted to do was get back to work and return to a state of normality. Or as close to it as I could manage, as I do not think that anything will ever seem normal again…

Glen was our link with the senior management that day, and was working hard for us as he had been all along and was trying to find out what we were going to be doing. The waiting around was having just as much of a negative effect on him as it was on the rest of us. He was getting frustrated with the lack of information that was coming our way and this was evident in the way he was acting. The normally quiet and reserved supervisor had become completely the reverse. It was clear that he was suffering from the events of the day before, too.

In the weeks and months to follow, I was to find out that it is easier to see the symptoms of trauma in others than it is in yourself. People that you know change in their mannerisms and moods overnight. If somebody has a negative trait then it becomes more severe; with me, it was my anger and foul mood swings. It shames me now, as things that have happened in my life since the bombings could have been avoided if I had been more aware of my own symptoms, but I know that I am not entirely at fault. We all have done things that we regret and mine is not asking for help sooner.

Eventually, Glen found out what our purpose was to be that day. We were again to go to King's Cross to see the Occupational Health team and get what I described at the time as 'A check-up from the neck up'. We managed to get a lift there in one of the mini buses that the force had rented to move officers to the cordons around the city and it was only a short journey to the Cross from where we are stationed. We went to the offices where the team had set themselves up and waited around for a while for them to prepare for us.

There were a lot more of us now. Officers had joined us who had worked at the other scenes and some officers that had worked at Russell Square, but who I do not remember seeing, were there as well. In all, there were about fifteen of us and we waited and joked around and waited and smoked and waited and moaned about the waiting.

We started to be called in about an hour later. There was a psychiatric nurse, a normal nurse to give us a quick check-up and also – to the amusement of us all – there was a masseuse to rub away at our tired muscles. Not being too keen about this kind of thing, I declined this last service, as did most others, but it gave us something else to joke about – and we needed something. The jokes were not in the best taste, but at least we were smiling and I felt a little more like myself. I was surrounded by people who were my friends, people that I had found a whole new respect for in the last 24 hours, who understood my pain when no one else could.

My turn came to see the psychiatric nurse and I walked into the office with a smile on my face because of a joke that had been cracked moments before. I sat in a chair still giggling and she introduced herself and what she hoped to achieve by seeing me. 'OK,' I thought, 'let's get this over with so I can go home.' She started asking me a lot of questions about what I had done, where I had been, what I was feeling and if I had been having disturbing images in my head or bad dreams the night before. My answers were all short and all the ones about my state of mind were a lie.

I did not mean to mislead anyone, especially this nice lady who only had my best interests at heart. But I was an ex-

British soldier, a police officer and I was a grown man. I did not show weakness to anybody, especially some stranger who would judge me on my answers. I had my pride and I was not going to open up to her.

I think back on this now and realise what an idiot I was being. These people were trying to help me and I was deceiving them on purpose to save face. I still think that this evaluation was a little soon after the event, as I was still in a state of shock and though I knew what I was feeling at that time, I should not have lied. It is possible that if I had been truthful with this woman, then I would have got help sooner and may not have ended up in the state that I did.

Next, I had to go and see the nurse, who took my blood pressure and made me blow into a bizarre contraption to test how my lungs were working. I took as big a lungful of air as I could, but basically ended up coughing into the tube. More of the horrible black stuff came up and I put it into a tissue that I had started carrying the night before. I think this told her all she needed to know, as she told me that I was suffering from smoke inhalation from the amount of time that I had spent in the tunnel. I still think to this day that the amount that I had smoked since the event was the main contributing factor. But I accepted her diagnosis as it meant that I got to go home.

I waited around for the others to finish up and we walked back to the station. The others had basically received a clean bill of health and had to stay at work. I felt really guilty about being the only one who had been released and hung around for ages after being told to leave. The others were being kept waiting and they still had all the uncertainty of what was going to happen to them. It was only when Glen found out that I was still there a couple of hours later that he ordered me home.

It was with a great sense of regret that I left my friends that day. They had experienced the same things as me and I had to leave them behind. Why should I be the only one going home? They were the only ones who knew what I was feeling at that time; just being around them made me feel better. We had an understanding – nothing needed to be said, it was an unconscious feeling of acceptance between us all that we would never be the same people that we were when we had turned up for work the day before, and I drew great comfort from this. I knew that I would know these officers for the rest of my life; we would share something that no one else could ever understand. We were the few and everyone else was an outsider.

I walked to Victoria this time. I did not fancy the Tube journey again after my experiences of that morning. The day was overcast but hot and it was not long before the humidity started to affect me and I began to sweat. The streets were not as busy as they should have been. It was around six o'clock on a Friday night and it should have been quite lively by that time. All the pubs and bars were open but I could see the staff standing round inside chatting, whereas normally they would have settled into the mad routine that is the West End on a Friday night in the height of summer.

I thought about getting a bus or a taxi, but despite the heat I was enjoying the walk that was taking me past all the famous landmarks that I had got so used to and usually took for granted. Centre Point, Cambridge Circus, Trafalgar Square, Admiralty Arch, Whitehall, Ten Downing Street, the Houses of Parliament, Westminster Abbey – my route took me past all of them. I found myself looking at them and appreciating them more than I ever had done before. I felt more a part of this great city than I had done previously and realised that all of these monuments were my heritage. I couldn't help but feel that I had done my part, as so many had before me, in preserving the sanctity of our nation's capital and those that live and work here. This city that has had such a turbulent past had just seen another chapter of its history opened and I had featured in it – something that gave me a great feeling of pride.

Chapter Thirteen

FRIENDS

My train journey home was fairly uneventful. As was becoming the norm with me, I fell into a waking dream and awoke an hour and twenty-five minutes later. This time had given me chance to think about my ordeal – something that had not had the best effect on me. I was down again and feeling very sorry for myself at the thought of having to go home and be on my own. There was only one thing for it; I had to go to my mum's. I needed to be around people, I did not want to think any more. I planned to get drunk.

I walked in the door and the scene that greeted me was a total contrast to the one from the night before. Most of my friends were in there and they all cheered me as I walked in. This still brings tears to my eyes when I think about it, even now. I was delighted and extremely embarrassed all at the same time. Two of my closest friends – Dave and Lisa – came up to me and gave me a huge hug. David is my oldest friend; we have known each other since we were very young and have remained close throughout our lives. Lisa is his partner of five years and is one of the nicest people that I have ever met. They complement each other completely and it seems that whenever I am down they are there to pick me back up again.

When my mobile phone had started working again the day before, I was bombarded with text messages and voice mails from people that I knew. A message from Dave was first in the queue. I do not think he realises how much he means to me, but I love him like a brother.

The year before, my wife of five years had left me. We had come to the end of our time together for many reasons, but I was holding on to her for dear life as she was the mother of my child and despite our problems I loved her desperately. When she left, she took my whole life away with her. My son Brook, who was nearly four at the time, was the centre of my world; he went with her and I was left in turmoil.

I was slipping at the time, slipping into a completely self-destructive cycle that would have seen me in ruins before Christmas came around. I was drinking all day every day, I wasn't eating, and I wasn't going to work. Dave and Lisa caught me, supported me, and put me back on my feet. I spent a lot of time with them in that period, much more than I had ever done before, and they accepted me as part of their lives. I do not think that they realise even now what their friendship meant to me at that time, but I am sure that it is what saved me from myself.

FRIENDS

Standing in the doorway of that pub, surrounded by my friends, it was all I could do to stop myself crying. Not crying because of my experiences the day before, but crying with the happiness I felt at the time. I was completely taken aback by it all. They all came up to me one or two at a time and gave me words of support or just a hug. It was fantastic. For those brief moments all my feelings of negativity and all the disturbing images in my mind were washed away. My friends were around me, I didn't have to worry about going to work and I was miles away from London. I could relax at last.

I changed at home after everyone had settled down and returned to the pub in record time. Even though I only had to be on my own for a short time, all the crap was sneaking back into my mind. I wanted to be around my friends, they were the ones that made it all go away. I wanted to see Dave and Lisa and thank them for being there for me once again.

I walked back into the pub and started to talk to everyone who was there and thank them for turning out, but at the same time I was trying to avoid talking about the events of the day before. I just wanted to be with them and try and have fun, but the subject kept coming up. They were not to know at the time what I had been through; none of them does to this day. I think that they have a fairly good idea, as the events of the day have been so widely publicised, but only a small amount of that information has come from me.

The people that know me best would tell you that I do not take praise well. I feel uncomfortable when I am given attention and shy away from any kind of situation that will put me in the spotlight for something that I have done. 'If it happens, fine; if I can avoid it, then that's better' is my general view. But I had become a minor celebrity in my mum's pub overnight and I couldn't avoid the questions.

The more people were talking about the events, however, the worse it was getting. A situation that had started out as the best thing that could have happened at the time was quickly turning into the worst. All this was being exacerbated by the amount I was drinking. People were buying me drinks and I was drinking them on an empty stomach. It was not long before I was quite drunk.

I couldn't handle this any more, I had to get out of that environment, I was losing control of my emotions and I was determined that no one should see me break down. I ran into the Gents toilet, closely followed by my friend Angie. She had been watching me from a distance and had seen me losing it bit by bit as the evening went on.

Angie and I had not known each other for long at this point. She had recently moved to the area and had found herself working behind the bar for my mum. We had hit it off almost instantly and spent a lot of time together going out drinking and having a laugh. We understood each other and enjoyed each other's company, but we hadn't had what I would call an emotionally close relationship up until this point. She has since become one of my dearest friends and has been there for me through all of my difficulties in the past year, as I have tried to be there for hers.

Angie found me in the Gents with my back against the wall, looking at the floor. I could feel her standing there but did not want to look at her, I couldn't let her see me lose it.

But she lifted up my chin and looked at my eyes. I was close to tears before, but now they were brimming and had started to roll down my cheeks. Angie just hugged me. She has this wonderful motherly quality about her that made me instantly feel at ease. I did at that point let myself go. I am not sure how long we stayed there for, me crying harder than I ever have done before and Angie just holding me. I was aware of people coming into room and then turning around again and leaving when they saw us. I know I was talking to her but I cannot remember what I said between sobs. I was thinking about Gill, about how hard I had tried to save her and how I had failed. As far as I was concerned, she was dead because I was not strong enough and I was torturing myself because of it. These feelings of regret and failure would be an overriding feature in my life from now on. They had finally surfaced, now they would dominate my every waking thought. I could not get the image of Gill out of my mind. I had failed and she was dead.

I finally pulled myself together and left the toilet. I had stopped crying very abruptly and straight away became very embarrassed about it. Now I needed to leave the pub before I made a fool out of myself again. Dave and Lisa were preparing to leave – they were going to a friend's birthday party and I asked if I could go with them. They said that I could and we left everybody behind in the pub. It was the best sentiment ever, all those people turning up for me, but it was clear that I couldn't handle it. So I snuck out with my friends and went to a party where I did not know anybody.

Looking back at this all now, it is clear how messed up I

was. I wanted to be around people but I did not want any attention. I needed not to think, but people's questions were bringing out images and memories that I did not want to deal with at that time. Dave and Lisa did not ask that of me, they were just there and that meant more than all the congratulations and praise that I could have ever received. Once again my friends were there for me at a pivotal point in my life and I cannot thank them enough for that.

Chapter Fourteen

NOT COPING

The weekend that followed was a bit of a blur. It mainly involved me going slowly mental. I tried everything to get the images out of my mind. I was drinking, I was going out, I was trying to be around people as much as I could, but for the main part my mind was still in that tunnel.

I wanted to forget, I wanted to put it out of my head so that I could at least rest, but it would not go away no matter how I tried. I could not sleep, I still hadn't eaten anything and I was chain-smoking.

I was getting the same flashbacks that I had had on the train. All it took was the slightest trigger and I would be transported back to that place at that time. It could be something as small as a news broadcast or the room being a little too hot. The reaction was physical as well as mental. I could smell that awful smell, taste the smoke and feel the oppressive heat. I would normally try and disappear somewhere private when this happened, but a couple of times I was snapped back to reality by a friend who had noticed that I had drifted off in mid-conversation.

I was showering four of five times a day because I felt dirty and I was sure that the smell of that day was clinging to my skin. I think that people noticed this odd behaviour but chose to let it pass, hoping that I would sort myself out in time.

I couldn't watch the TV because every time the news came on it was about that day. I couldn't read the paper; I was a total wreck. I only slept out of exhaustion, and when I did my sleep was broken and dominated by nightmares so real that when I woke it took me a while to realise that I was still on my mum's sofa and not two hundred feet under the ground slipping on other people's blood.

After the counselling that I have had since, I know that my mind was trying to make sense of what I had gone through. I had taken in so much traumatic information in those three hours that my brain could not have possibly processed it properly.

When the brain takes information in at its own leisurely pace, it has the chance to file it away properly. It understands what it has seen and learnt and can cope. But when the brain is exposed to an event as traumatic as the 7 July bombings and all I had to endure during that day, it can't. It still takes the information in, but it just stuffs it in a corner. All the information is left as being sensory, the raw information as the brain has not had the time to process and understand it.

I have been told since that the dreams and the flashbacks

were just my mind trying to understand what had happened to me. It was digging out the jumbled information and sorting through it so that it could be filed away in the part of my mind that stores all the information and memories.

The physical reactions that I was getting at the time were part of this. Because I was thinking about these things, consciously or not, my brain was telling my body to prepare itself to go through that experience again. The reaction was programmed into me as an automated response to danger; it did not matter if that danger was real or just perceived.

I came by all this information much later on my road to recovery, it has helped me understand that my reaction was normal and that once my brain had worked through all the information that I would not get all these unwanted images and dreams. But I did not know any of this back then. I thought that I was just going mad and so I suppressed those images as best as I could. I did not want to think about any of it. This was the worst thing that I could have done.

On the Monday, I was phoned by the manager of our Human Resources department. Normally, she appears to be a very stern woman who takes no shit from anyone, but to my surprise she was very nice to me. I had expected her to demand that I return to work immediately. But she told me that I should take as long as I needed to rest and to come back to work when I was ready. She also said that all the others that had worked with me that day had been sent home with the same advice. This made me very happy and relieved a lot of the pressure that I felt at the time. I still felt guilty about being off when the others were back at work and had been previously been planning to return the next day, but at least now I had some time.

I phoned Gary the instant she had put down the phone. It had been my intention to ask him to come and stay with me for a few days so that we could go out on the beer. I still felt that the people I had worked with were the only ones that understood me at the time and I wanted to be around them. But when Gary picked up his phone it was clear that he was anywhere but at home. The background noise was unbelievable and I could barely hear him.

I asked him where he was and he told me that he was at work and that he was standing on a cordon outside Liverpool Street Station. In an instant, I was furious. I listened to him for a while and he told me that Glen had been sent home the night before, as he had clearly been affected by the incident, but now there was no one to fight their corner. The majority of them had gone back into work as usual and had been sent all over town to do jobs directly related to the incident.

After I had finished my conversation with Gary, I was straight back on the phone to Human Resources. I spoke to the same woman, but the tone of the conversation had changed dramatically. I was now laying down the law as far as I was concerned. Why were my friends still at work? Why were they not being cared for as I was? Why were they all at the scenes of the bombings? The woman was very calm with me, much more so than I deserved at the time. It was clear that she did not have a clue that this had happened and she told me that she would sort it as soon as possible.

I must have sounded like a raving lunatic. This woman must have been under so much pressure at work and I was just adding to her worries. The task of keeping track of resources must have been immense in the confusion that followed the disaster and it was not surprising that a few officers had slipped through the net. But as I was to find out, she was true to her word, when Gary phoned me an hour later they had all been sent home.

I spent the next week trying to get a grip on reality and suppress my feelings and the images of the event. On the whole, I did this quite successfully. I could function pretty normally on the exterior; it was only inside that the turmoil continued.

It was my view at the time that as long as everyone else thought I was OK then I would sort my own head out in time. My grief had become a very private affair. I had moved back to my flat on my own and tried to bottle everything up until I got home.

I was still bumping into people who would congratulate me on my efforts and generally making a fuss, but I felt that these people knew absolutely nothing. They were congratulating me on my efforts? Why? A woman had died, I had failed, I was not strong enough, I didn't think quickly enough. I was not a fucking hero I was a FUCK-UP!

I had found that I was reliving Gill's rescue attempt more than any other aspect of that day. I was dissecting everything I had done in that tunnel, thinking how I could have done better, how I could have run instead of walking, how I could have carried her so I could have kept a better grip on her, but most of all how I should have stayed with her until the end. I had just left her in the booking hall of that station with a paramedic who looked like a rabbit caught in the headlights.

I was torturing myself. There is no other description for what I was doing. I had never had anyone die on me before. I had been to a lot of incidents where people had died, but I had only been there to deal with the situation and pick up the pieces. This was different: this woman, this poor innocent, had been relying on me to save her and I couldn't. If someone else had been there in my place, someone stronger, would she have survived? This was a question that I asked myself incessantly.

But it didn't matter to me what I was feeling at this time. I was not going to expose my feelings and concerns to anyone else. They were my problem and mine to deal with alone.

Chapter Fifteen

BACK TO THE COAL FACE

I had spoken to Gary and the other guys that I worked with throughout the week that I had off. We were all concerned for each other. I think now that this was because we all knew what we were going through as individuals and empathised with one another as a result. Gary told me that he planned to go back to work on the Wednesday and although I still did not feel ready to go back I felt that same old sense of guilt so I made the decision to go back the day after him.

This was a big mistake, as will become apparent later. I was still in a right old mess and now I was planning to go back to work and try and do my job as I would have before all this happened. Not to mention the fact that most of our work is done on the Underground. What was I thinking?

My return to work was not a smooth one. I walked in the

door that Thursday morning, a week to the day after the bombings, not feeling my best after another Tube nightmare on the way in. As usual, though, I was determined that no one should see me being weak, so I acted as normally as I could.

I had told the lady in the Human Resources department that I would only go back to work if I did not have to do work that had anything to do with the bombings. I wanted to be out and about doing normal duties with my normal friends and arresting normal bad guys. She said that was fair and that she would talk to my supervisors about it.

Another team was working when I went in that afternoon. All the shifts were up in the air and people were being put everywhere at any time to work ridiculous hours. All the officers there looked tired and demoralised and I started to feel guilty for not having been at work for the previous week.

I sat at a computer and logged myself on to the system. You have to tell Big Brother that you are there so he can keep an eye on you. With this done, I made idle chat with the other team, as I was a bit early for my lot to have arrived.

It was at this point that their team sergeant walked in. He had that worried look of a supervisor that was in a bit of a pickle. He started to complain that the force had run out of officers to man the cordons. The officers that had worked one scene could not work at another because of cross-contamination issues to do with forensics. As a result, he was looking for replacements. His eyes settled on me. The conversation went something like this.

Sergeant: 'Have you been to Russell Square, Aaron?'

Me: 'Er, yes.'

Sergeant: 'Then grab your stuff, you are going back down there on the cordon.'

Me (enraged): 'You can fuck right off if you think I'm going back down there, you twat!'

Sergeant: 'You can't speak to me like that, I'm your superior. I'm going to the inspector about you.'

Me: 'I do not give a flying fuck who you are, if you think I am going back to that station then you are very wrong, my friend.'

I had flipped, fallen at the first hurdle. I had been at work for five minutes and already I had lost the plot with someone. The man did not know what I had been through at that station the week before. He had all the pressure of the world bearing down on his shoulders and I had told him to fuck off. Nice one, Aaron, why not go and kick the inspector in the shins as well just to let everyone know for sure that you are cracking up?

All the officers in the room were sitting in stunned silence and I was shaking with rage. I just couldn't prevent myself from bursting out like that. I walked out of the room without saying a word, went out of the front of the station to the park, had a cigarette and calmed myself down. I thought about what I said and done and regretted it deeply.

I went back upstairs, walked into the office of the supervisor concerned and apologised to him. I explained what I had been through, how I was only meant to be doing normal duties and how the last thing that I needed to do was go back to that station. He accepted my apology and even asked if I felt OK to work, adding that he had spoken to the inspector who had put it back in his hands to deal with, but as I had apologised to him without prompting, he was prepared to let it slide.

When the rest of my team arrived, we went about our normal day-to-day work and it went without incident, really. The only thing that was out of place was the fact that Glen was missing. I would not see him in over a month.

London was still very quiet, people were still coming into work, but the tourists were staying away. I was happy, though: I was driving around in circles talking to my radio operator and generally feeling normal for the first time in a week.

The guy that I was working with that day had also been on duty on the day of the bombings, but he had been at a different scene. We talked about our experiences in brief – nothing too detailed, but we spent most of our time moaning about how we had been treated since. I did not really have much to say in that respect, but joined in anyway as obviously the other officer felt quite strongly about the whole thing.

This was to be the norm now for the week that followed, I would go to work as usual, and not do much of anything apart from be there in body. My mind was still somewhere completely different, but I do not think that anyone could tell. I was like a magician: I could be hiding all sorts up my sleeve and no one would ever know unless I chose to show them.

London remained on a very high state of alert. Everyone was still very on edge and this was reflected in the calls we were taking. The amount of unattended items reported at train stations went through the roof. It seemed like we were spending the majority of the time evacuating stations and waiting for the all clear from the guys who worked on the bomb car. I thought that it was highly irresponsible of commuters to continue to be so neglectful about their belongings after all that had happened, but it was still occurring and we were still attending.

I'll just quickly explain to you what the bomb car is before I proceed. Basically, it is two officers in a Renault people carrier who whizz around London going to suspect package calls and unattended items. They carry lots of cool kit like x-ray machines and electromagnetic field detectors and they get to declare whether the suspected item is or is not an explosive device. They do have other functions, but those are not really relevant to my story so I'll leave it at that.

Some time in the week that followed, the force organised for us all to have a proper psychological evaluation. Now that things had calmed themselves down and the scenes were running smoothly, we were to take our turn in getting sorted out. The organisation wanted to know exactly what the state of play was with all of us as individuals and as a result get us any help that we needed.

The evaluation was at our area headquarters in St James's Park, near the Houses of Parliament. My appointment was made and I attended in good spirits. I was confident that I could get through it without being deemed mental.

Arriving fashionably late, as per usual, I walked into one of the conference rooms, where a woman from an Occupational Health firm was waiting for me. We made some introductions and she told me the purpose of the interview was to evaluate me and to determine whether I was suffering from post-traumatic stress disorder.

I had heard of this condition before. We had been told about it when I was with the army. But we all thought it to be a complete load of shite then. My opinion of it now remained the same. Why should it alter? This was only something that affected weak people who couldn't handle the situations that they faced. It didn't even come into the picture where I was concerned: I was dealing with this on my own and I was doing fine – apart from the flashbacks, the nightmares, the physical reactions and the overwhelming guilt that I carried about the death of Gill. Fucking tree-hugging hippy shrinks. They didn't know anything about me.

That was my opinion of post-traumatic stress disorder back then. It certainly is not now. If I had told any of the people that were trying to help me what I was really thinking, then I might not have ended up like I am now. This is a big regret for me now – the biggest, I think.

The nice lady asked me to tell her what I had done on the day and I regurgitated the same story that I had told to everyone who had asked previously. I had managed to give people a brief summary of what I had done without it having any effect on me whatsoever. The story touched no sore points. It was literally something to give people so that I could get away with not showing any emotion and it worked every time.

With the initial bit out of the way, she started to ask me questions. These were a little harder to defend myself against:

104

they were quite probing and some came close to getting through my barriers. I had made the mistake of mentioning Gill and she seemed to be focusing in on that. Perhaps she wasn't such a nice woman after all.

It had become clear that I had to defend myself against this person and her questions, but I didn't want to seem overly evasive. I took my time in answering her, all the time considering my answers carefully. I was giving her a little but not enough for her to think that I was remotely mental.

It was a game for me, a serious one. I could not be sent home again. I could not be left on my own so that the images could creep back into my mind. I needed to be at work where my mates were, where I could occupy myself easily without having to think about it, I needed to drown myself in it and that is exactly what I had planned to do. This woman and her all-powerful clipboard were not going to stand in my way.

I walked out of that building with a clean bill of health and a smile on my face. I had pulled the wool over everyone's eyes. Wasn't I a genius?

You may be reading this and thinking that I am a complete idiot – and you would be right. But what I would like you to understand at this point is that being at work was the only thing that had made me feel remotely normal since the event. Day in and day out I was dealing with beggars, shoplifters and drunks. These were as far removed from terrorists and bombs as you could get and I was soaking it up. I was on fire; I was taking more calls and making more arrests than most other officers and it felt good. I could not be taken off active duty and be sent home – or worse, be put behind a desk. This would be torture for me at the best of times, but at this point I was scared that my thoughts of that day would consume me and drive me mad.

I continued as normal after that interview. The organisation was happy that I was sane and I was happy that I was at work. Everything was going according to plan for me. All I had to do now was sort my head out. Easy: I'll just bury it so deep it will never surface again. Crisis over and time to pick up the pieces and move on with our lives. I would manage – I always did.

Neither I, nor anyone else, was to know that someone somewhere felt that not enough death and destruction had happened. And the day after my appointment in St James's Park, they tried to do it all again.

Chapter Sixteen

21 JULY 2005

I was at home asleep on my sofa when my phone rang. I remember being pissed off with myself for not turning it off the night before; I still wasn't sleeping well and had only been dozing for a few hours. The TV was still on, the film that I had been watching long since over. I had slept on my sofa for nearly two weeks now. I did not have a TV in my bedroom and I needed to have my mind occupied until the point of exhaustion and falling asleep. Not ideal, I know, but it worked and I didn't have to think.

I looked at my phone and saw that it was a text message from a friend at work. I opened it, and read the three words: WATCH THE NEWS! 'Bollocks, what now?' I thought. So I turned my TV onto SKY News. And was instantly horrified.

The first thing that I saw was police cordons everywhere, ambulances, and fire engines. It had happened again. I had no control over it, I was back there again, but this time it was stronger and more vivid that it had ever been before. I lost time to this one. I have no memory of being in my front room any more I was literally transported back in time two weeks and dumped in front of that fucking train towering over me in the dark.

When I snapped myself out of it and had stuffed all that shit back into the farthest reaches of my mind, I had a cigarette. I was soaked through with sweat and was shaking uncontrollably. I wasn't even in London and I had flipped out at the thought of those events happening again. After a bit, I focused my attention on the television and began to get a better idea of what had happened and what I was seeing.

Suicide bombers had attacked the transport system again, but the devices had failed to initiate. Thank God. I do not know much detail about what actually happened, as I avoided all the news stories about it. It all just served to remind me of my situation.

I think that one of the devices was at Oval, one at Warren Street and I think that the bus was in Shepherd's Bush. Another device had been dumped and found near to a prison in north London. I cannot be totally sure about all of this – I just didn't want to know the details at the time.

I have heard since that the detonators that the suspects used were not powerful enough to set off the explosives that they were carrying that day. There was a small explosion from the detonators, enough to shatter the windows on the trains and the bus but not enough power in them to initiate the entire device.

I hate to say that I was right, but thinking back two weeks before this I had predicted another attack during a conversation with a friend at work. I was looking at a Tube map at the time and was trying to work out the logic in the placement of the first attack's devices. The idea of a terrorist attack is to cause as much fear and disruption as possible. All the attacks were in the north and east of London. The bombers had come into town at King's Cross and attacked targets close to or directly accessible from there.

To me, this did not seem to add up. The terrorists had caused a massive amount of damage, loss of life and disruption, but they had not brought London to the standstill that surely would have been their ultimate aim. As I have said before, I had used the Tube to get to work the next day and the buses were running all day, so London was far from being at a standstill. In commuting terms, the Tube lines that closed as a result of the attacks were just an inconvenience, not a crippling blow.

My hunch was that there would be other attacks, one in the south and the west, in contrast to the attack in the north and the east. But it was just a hunch, there were people much more highly qualified and paid to think about this type of thing than me. I thought at the time that I was just worrying for the sake of doing so.

No one was seriously hurt and things were under control very quickly. There was none of the drama of the previous incident and for that we all should be thankful.

I wish I had more to say about this, but at the time I tried to shut it out as best I could. I was at home, I was going on to night shifts the day after, and I would deal with it then. For now at least I was going to the pub and I was going to get drunk.

Work phoned me when I was in the pub. I had been in there all day and was trying to sound as sober as I could. They asked me if I wanted to go into work and earn a bit of double time working on the cordons at the new scenes. I politely declined and explained that while I had only had 'a few' I would not risk driving to London. Leaving them satisfied with my answer, I went about the tasks of forgetting and chatting up the barmaids.

I went into work the next night as I had planned, but my journey was a frustrating one. This latest incident certainly caused a lot of disruption, if only for a short time.

The Piccadilly Line, the Hammersmith and City Line and the Circle Line were all closed because of the 7 July attacks. But now the Victoria Line, the Central Line and the Northern Line were closed too. This is what I meant by bringing the London transport system to a stop. If that second wave of devices had detonated, the city would have been crippled for months.

I ended up getting a bus to work. When I arrived at the station, things were mad. The strains being placed on manpower had literally doubled overnight. The force was having trouble finding resources for all its commitments after the attacks on the 7th. Now they had three more crime scenes to guard and investigate.

The way they had got round this was to recruit officers from all over the country on short-term contracts. These officers would be paid at the full London rate plus an allowance for being away from home, free accommodation and expenses. Those that volunteered were going to make a fortune off the government.

Officers had started arriving from everywhere. As well as British Transport Police from Wales, Scotland and the Midlands there were officers from the county forces from Liverpool, Manchester and Birmingham. All these officers were badly needed and lightened the burden on officers from London who had been working their behinds off for the last fortnight.

My night shift was an easy one. We were not at all busy, it was a Friday night, and this was strange to say the least. Driving around the West End that night it felt like midweek. Everywhere was open, but there were just no people around.

I was working on my own that night. A few officers were still off because of the bombings and several more had been put onto cordon duties. We were really thin on the ground, but it seemed not to matter as we were not getting many calls.

I stopped at one of my regular coffee stops in Leicester Square for a chat and a drink. I knew the owners well because I had chucked a few drunks out of there in the past. We were on first-name terms and they were always really nice to me.

I liked doing things like this at work. Getting to know the people that work daily in your area is what it is all about, really. They like having police officers around their establishments, especially at night; it means that they do not get as much trouble and we get a warm greeting and a good chat about what has been happening in the area.

The owners of this coffee house were not in such good spirits that night, though. When I asked them why, they told me that business had been really bad for the previous few weeks after the bombings. They told me that the tourist trade had almost died completely and the Friday and Saturday trade had been almost non-existent. I felt really sorry for them – they shouldn't be suffering because of this. They were really nice people, Muslims.

I drove around in aimless circles for most of the night. I stopped in at a few of the West End stations to say hello to the staff, but they all had the same story to tell as the owners of the coffee house. How long was this going to last? Surely people wouldn't stay away forever?

During the course of my aimless driving, I stumbled upon a hen party shouting and screaming their way through Covent Garden. They were the only ones that I had seen all night who looked completely relaxed and oblivious to what had gone on recently. I smiled to myself and planned to drive on. But they spotted me.

There is nothing more attractive to a hen party of middle-aged women than a young police officer in full uniform. The hen ran right up to the van and planted a big kiss on my cheek. I blushed and tried to say something witty but failed miserably. She was really pretty and I've always been a sucker for a pretty woman. I started making small talk with her, chatting her up and generally having a laugh doing what I like to call 'force relations'. She was a nice woman and had my full attention. Big mistake on my part, because the next thing I knew the passenger door and the rear sliding door of the van had been opened and the other seven members of the hen party had joined me in the van.

I had to laugh – I could do nothing else. In the end, I had to bribe them out of my van by promising them all a kiss and agreeing to let them have their photo taken with me wearing my hat. It's a difficult life policing the West End of London some nights…!

I would like to tell you lots of exciting stories about all the amazing jobs that I dealt with in the following week, but I cannot. London was a virtual ghost town at night compared to what it is usually like. I couldn't help feeling sorry for the small businesses, like that coffee house, which were suffering because of the lack of trade.

Chapter Seventeen

ANGER

I think that now it is appropriate to talk about my feelings towards the individuals who detonated the devices on 7 July and killed themselves along with 52 others. I have avoided talking about it until this point because during the weeks and months that followed the attacks I did not know what to think.

On the day of the bombings I was not sure what had happened on those trains. Although a suicide bombing was the main theory among all those that attended, we could not be one hundred per cent sure about it.

When it was first confirmed that the carnage was indeed the work of suicide bombers, I was furious. The thought of those men blowing themselves up and killing all those innocent people made my blood boil. I thought that they were psychopaths. They had walked into our beloved capital and irreversibly changed the lives of hundreds, if not thousands, of people.

They were selfish, they were hateful and they were twisted. I couldn't fathom it; I could not work out why in God's name they would want to do something so horrendous. There had not even been any warning, not even a codeword as the IRA used to use. There was nothing until all those people were dead.

And what about me? What the fuck had I done to deserve being exposed to all that horror? Why should I have had to pay the price for their beliefs? They had stolen my innocence. I had seen what no living person should have to and it had left me in tatters.

When I saw their four faces on the TV, I wanted to smash the screen. When I saw their families and friends expressing their dismay at what had happened, I thought they were lying. I hated everything about them. But then I listened to the words of one of these bombers and my views started to change.

I was sitting at home chilling out after a shift at work. It was daft o'clock in the morning and there was nothing on, so I was watching the news. One of the features was a video released by one of the bombers. I think it was the guy from Edgware Road, Mohammad Sidique Khan. As soon as his face came on the TV, I started hating him instantly, he was a multiple murderer, he had caused pain and suffering to so many and he deserved to burn in the deepest bowels of hell. But then he started to speak and I couldn't help but stop hating him and starting to feel sorry for him.

He sounded like a robot. He was a pre-programmed

machine. He was young, only 30 years old. He was a victim, a stupid fool who was influenced by a few… I saw him as weak, weak in spirit – he couldn't think for himself. The more I listened, the more certain I was of my pity for him – for all four of them.

The more I listened, the more I was sure of this. He had been picked out by fundamentalists because he was young and impressionable. They had taken him and his friends to one side and shown them all sorts of horrible images and propaganda and brainwashed them into thinking that the West was the enemy.

I do not know that much about Islam as a religion, but I know that Muslims are a peaceful people and that killing innocents is forbidden by their holy book, the Koran. These few fundamentalists do not represent the views of most Muslims, they just prey on the weak and use them as tools in their evil campaign.

From what I can gather, the breakaway factions have twisted the teachings of their holy book and declared a holy war on the governments of the West. Apparently the West is encroaching on their homelands because of our so-called arrogance and insatiable greed for natural resources. The West is undermining their way of life and polluting their culture with 'evil western' ways. As a result of all this, these factions think it reasonable to attack our cities and kill innocent people without conscience. They see us all as targets, as we are infidels.

I have never heard so much rubbish in all my life. How can we, as normal people, be blamed for the actions of our governments? It's difficult for us even to influence them about affairs that directly concern us at home, let alone about foreign policy. We are just trying to get along like everyone else in the world. Why should we be blown up on our way to work?

I have nothing but contempt for the people that organise these fundamentalist groups. They are ruining the reputation of their religion and ruining the lives of young and impressionable people. I feel sorry for those that fall under their spell. They have their heads filled with so many lies and so much hate that they are left with no choices. They are promised everything but end up with nothing. They leave behind loving families and in some cases even their young children. All because they were made to believe something that somebody else told them about places that most have not been to.

All these four young British Muslims achieved in the end was death and destruction and shame to their faith. They are not martyrs, they are murderers. They took the lives of 52 innocent people and maimed countless others – to prove what? I am not a religious man by any definition of the word, so I do not think that they died gloriously, went to meet their god and were surrounded by virgins. I believe that they ended up like everybody else: in bits. A total waste of life and to top it off, they will not have gone down in history as martyrs, they will be remembered by most of us as murderers. They did not die a glorious death, they died horribly, like everybody else.

I am sure the video that poor lad recorded was designed to strike fear into our hearts, but personally it only made me pity him. How can I be angry with someone who has had his choices taken away from him? How can I be angry at a young man who thought that he was a soldier and that he was fighting a war?

I was a soldier and I can tell you that these individuals were nothing of the sort. As a solider, you must have a moral obligation and a respect for the lives of non-combatants. It has been outlined in the rules of war time after time, throughout the whole history of the civilised world, that civilians should not be harmed. It is one thing to fight for what you believe in, but it is another to strike out randomly and viciously at innocent people. These are not the actions of soldiers but of terrorists; there was no honour in what they did, it was murder pure and simple.

I know that my knowledge of Islam and the workings of fundamentalist groups must seem limited, and that is because it is. I know enough to understand what has gone on and form my own views, though. I have spent my entire adult life dealing with terrorism and I know that terrorists are all the same. They are disillusioned cowards who have not got the backbone to come out of the shadows.

This event has turned me into a bit of a pacifist, what I would have previously have referred to as a 'tree hugger'. It has made me question my government's foreign policy and their motivation for taking part in recent conflicts. I am in no way justifying the actions of the bombers, though I believe that we must alter the way we are dealing with the situation. But how do we go back? Our country is reliant on the resources that the Arab states possess. The government would have us believe that we only invaded Iraq because Saddam

Hussein was a tyrant and was oppressing his people and so on, but this simply is not the case. There are atrocities going on in the world that are on a par with what was happening in Iraq and worse, but do we invade all those countries and replace their governments? No, we do not. Why? Because they are poor and have nothing that we want, they have little or no natural resources, so why should we care?

We didn't invade Rwanda when the genocide was taking place there. The UN sent a handful of troops but they were powerless to do anything but watch the atrocities happen. We took a little more interest in Sierra Leone, but they had diamonds. The coalition of Britain and the United States had never before seen it necessary to break ranks with the UN and engage in a full military action despite all the horrific events going on elsewhere around the globe. Why now?

My background as a soldier meant that I was formerly always up for a good war. It was glorious, it created heroes; we could flex our muscles as a nation and strike fear into our enemies. If I had have gone to war, I would have been spectacular and, if I had died, I would have been remembered and been among the honoured dead. I would have died for my country and for the greater good. Who do I sound like now? You see, I too was brainwashed. I can relate to how the 7 July bombers came to believe the things that they did, but just because I can relate to it does not mean that I understand it or condone it. It's just that I realise now how easy it is to be blind.

Chapter Eighteen

THE ARMY

I can remember the exact time and place that I decided I didn't want to be a soldier in the British army any more. I think that this was the biggest turning point in my life and started the chain of events that led me to being on duty that morning in July 2005. I was in the middle of Salisbury Plain on an exercise with my regiment; it was 11 September 2001.

It was a foul morning; I was absolutely freezing cold and had just been out running communication wire between our defensive positions in the company harbour. We had been on the go for days and I had had hardly any sleep. We had been moving from position to position, permanently on the go and only stopping to engage the mock enemy. I was dead on my feet.

It had taken me a couple of hours to complete my task. I had been out in the cold since first light and was absolutely gagging for a cigarette, a cup of tea and maybe the chance of getting my head down for an hour or two.

I made my way back to my vehicle, the command Saxon armoured personnel carrier, to drop off my kit, but when I arrived I saw a large group of my mates standing around the wagon. This was unheard of and a big no-no in the field. We were tactically competing with a live enemy. Everyone should have been in their positions, keeping low and sorting out their personal administration while they had the chance.

As I moved closer, I could see that they were all crowded around a small black-and-white TV that had been rigged up to the generator by the company signaller. This normally only came out for *Match of the Day* and *EastEnders*. Why was it out now, when everyone should have been as busy as me?

Out of curiosity, I looked over somebody's shoulder – just in time to see the second passenger plane plough into the World Trade Center.

At first, I refused to believe that this had actually happened and asked the guy next to me if this was a film, but as soon as the picture switched back to the news room and I started listening to the newsreader, the reality of it sank in. I stood there with my mouth open and gaped at the scene.

I was thousands of miles from that event, but I was staggered by the magnitude of it. This was a massive deal. I have always been interested in world affairs, and of course they were an integral part of my life at the time. In that instant, I realised that life in the armed forces had just changed forever.

It was obvious to me right at the start that the chances of

being deployed to a war zone had just gone through the roof. There was going to be a war on terror and the British army was going to be in the front line. I couldn't be a part of that for many reasons – most of all because I didn't want to risk my life.

To some of you this may sound a little cowardly, but it wasn't as if I had never been to a war zone before. I did operational tours of Northern Ireland and Bosnia, but this was a whole different kettle of fish. I knew that the consequences would involve operations in the Middle East to target terrorism at the grass roots and that was not at the time an appealing prospect.

I could not stop thinking of what happened to the Russians when they went into Afghanistan and the America's involvement in Vietnam. I knew that this whole ordeal would turn into an attempt by the West to go into the Middle East and finish the job that it failed to do in the early 1990s. It was all about oil then and it is all about oil now. It would be the common soldiers who paid the ultimate price for their parent country's greed; it would all go horribly wrong and I was not going to be a part of it. I would not lay my life on the line for someone else's hidden agenda.

I had a young family at the time; I was newly married with a five-year-old stepson and a son of my own who wasn't even a year old. I could not risk putting myself in the firing line of their sake. What would happen to them if I were deployed for a long period of time? Or what would happen to them if I were to become seriously injured, or even killed? It was not a risk that I thought I could take.

★ ★ ★ ★ ★

It was not an easy decision for me to leave the army. It had been my home since I left school and the life had been good to me in the five years preceding the events in New York. I had travelled the world and had some fantastic life experiences, but I never thought for one second that leaving the army would ultimately lead to me being on the front line of the biggest terrorist attack in mainland Britain.

The army had been a way out for me in the beginning. I was not happy at home, because I did not have a good relationship with my mother at the time and I had left school with virtually no qualifications.

The nature of my relationship with my mum really stemmed from the fact that we moved around a lot when we were kids. She never seemed to be happy in any of her relationships and was married and divorced three times by the time I was 11. I do not think any ill of her because of this now, but when I was younger it felt like my sister and I were being dragged along in her wake and that we were more of a burden to her than anything else. I learnt from an early age that I could not rely on anyone and that the only person that looks after you is yourself.

As a result of these feelings, I was very detached from anything emotional when I was a kid. I didn't know how to relate to people properly or express my emotions in a healthy way. This led to me becoming a very angry young man and more than a bit of a rogue.

When I was a little older, in secondary school, I was a real handful. I was always in trouble of some description, more often or not because of my fists. I would cause trouble and fight just to get some attention and I can only guess at how much stress I put my mum under. I wouldn't attend classes and thought of school as a bit of a social event more than anything else.

When I left school it finally hit home that I had wasted my education. A lot of my friends were going to college and getting apprenticeships, but I had nothing. No one had bothered suggesting any form of further education to me, because I was such a lost cause. I probably wouldn't have listened anyway. I had no qualifications, no job and no prospects; I didn't know what to do.

My mum and I had been going through a really bad patch because of the situation that I have just described and one day she went as far as to kick me out of the house. I found myself wandering around the streets of Canterbury the day after as a very troubled young man. It was then that I noticed the front window of the Army recruiting office and saw all the posters of soldiers wind-surfing and scuba-diving. Then next thing I knew, I was signing the bottom of an application that the recruiting officer had led me through.

A few months later I was in and never looked back. The training was hard, but the discipline was the worst. I had to go from being a bit of a rebel to being a disciplined infantry soldier. Needless to say, I slipped up a few times and spent more than my share of time in the guard house being punished, but I got through it in the end. By the time that I had finished my basic training I had done so many punishment push-ups that I could bang out thirty using only one arm!

When I eventually left the army in 2002, I didn't have a clue what I was going to do with myself. I wanted to join the police, but the application and selection process seemed too long winded. I had sent out applications for every police force that I could think of. I knew I wanted to work in or just outside London, so I had applied to all of the home county forces, the Metropolitan Police, the City of London Police and the British Transport Police.

It was simply because the Transport Police responded first that I ended up where I am today. I was so keen to be a police officer, I thought that the police would be an easy transition for me. It was a disciplined service and I really thought it would be a walk in the park.

I found training for the police quite a challenge. It wasn't the academic stuff that was the difficulty, it was the political correctness that is inherent in the organisation that I had a problem dealing with. I was your stereotypical squaddie. I was loud, brash and very gobby. I never thought before I opened my mouth and I landed myself in hot water more than a few times by not thinking before I spoke. I learnt very quickly that the environment was nothing like the army and I had to work really hard to solve the problem of my mouth running away with me.

When I was a squaddie, every other word out of my mouth was an obscenity or a remark about something that if I heard it now would make me cringe. Saying something like that on the job in the police is potentially a sacking offence; I had to completely review my colourful vocabulary and start afresh. It was worth the effort, though. From the moment that I first walked out onto the street as a brand, spanking-new police officer, I knew that I had made the right decision. I loved interacting with people and all the challenges that the job provided. I was hooked.

I was posted to the Underground in the centre of London as a rapid-response officer. It was my job to read the map and talk on the radio while the driver took care of the business of driving on the blue lights through the busy streets of central London. I couldn't have hoped for a job that I enjoyed more and I like to think that I took to it like a duck to water.

Working in London, I found myself in a situation that was very focused on terrorism. I wouldn't say that I never took it seriously, but I think that I was a little more laid back about it than some other officers. I had been to Northern Ireland, after all, and was an old hat at all this terrorist business. I wasn't worried about it at the time. The thought that terrorists would attack London would have seemed outrageous.

When I look back at all this now, it makes me realise how important the decisions we make are: one small choice can lead to a chain of events that has the potential to change your life forever. As I have already said, I left the armed forces to remove the possibility of going abroad, fighting for something that I didn't believe in and facing the possibility of getting injured or worse. But all that happened is that I ended up dealing with the situation anyway – not halfway round the world in a strange country, but in my nation's capital. My colleagues and I had to work in the most despicable of conditions to salvage what life we could after that cowardly act of terrorism. I'm not sure if I would have seen worse overseas or not.

Chapter Nineteen

FRONT-PAGE NEWS

I had been back at work for about three weeks now. Things were going well. I was still working all the hours that I could get and I was still out there arresting bad guys and keeping the transport system safe. No one at work or at home had any idea about what was going on in my head and I was happy about that. It meant that I could stay at work and keep myself busy.

When I was on my own, things were still very bad. I was not sleeping for more than two hours a night. I had lost nearly two stone because I was not eating, but I had been telling everyone that I had joined the gym. My nightmares and flashbacks were still very bad and sometimes, when I got a really bad one, I would zone out for significant periods of time. But all this was OK, because I felt I was in control; I would sort myself out.

My guilt about the death of Gill was crippling. It dominated my waking thoughts and was the theme of all my bad dreams. I had been scouring the casualty lists, looking at the names of the dead and trying to work out which one she was. At the time, I wanted to contact her family to tell them that I was sorry for letting their loved one die. It was bad and I can only admit that now. Her death was tearing me up inside. But my grief and guilt was invisible to everyone except myself.

All this aside, I could still function as well as I ever did at work. My supervisors were pleased with the work I was turning out and I was pleased because my plan was working. I was pulling the wool over everyone's eyes and I thought it wouldn't be long now before all the pain went away.

It was right at the end of July that I had my first real test at work since the bombings. As I have said before, all the jobs that we were dealing with were low-level stuff and not very challenging, but this day would be different.

It was a hot day and I was cruising around Hyde Park enjoying the weather. My operator that day was an officer called Andy, a young lad in his early twenties. He is hysterically funny and very intelligent. He always has a joke, normally at someone else's experience, and is good fun to work with. I also have a lot of respect for Andy as an officer: he is sharp thinker and reacts to a situation quickly.

Andy and I were bored. Nothing had happened all shift and we were gagging for a good job to come along. Then over the radio came the message 'ANY UNIT TO ATTEND HOLLAND PARK LU STATION,

DISTURBANCE ON A TRAIN, TRAIN BEING HELD ON THE PLATFORM'. This was technically out of our area, but Andy and I were so bored we took the call. We were on Park Lane at the time.

I switched on the blues and twos, accelerated and started weaving my way through the traffic. I wasn't going as fast as I could have, but the call didn't sound too serious at this time. It was probably just a couple of commuters declaring handbags at dawn because one had trod on the other's little toe.

Then the controller announced, 'UPDATE FROM HOLLAND PARK, MALE WITH A HAMMER ATTACKING PASSENGERS, STATION BEING EVACUATED.' 'Shit!' was the first thing that went through my mind. I looked at Andy and he had a very worried look on his face. The day was just about to get a whole lot more interesting.

The drive there was easy, a straight route all the way down the Bayswater Road. But I had just had a massive adrenaline dump and was on a mission. We were flying. I didn't look at the speedo in the car but I would guess that at points we were doing over eighty miles per hour. The drive was flawless and we arrived at Holland Park less than two minutes after receiving the call.

I dumped, rather than parked, the car outside and Andy and I ran into the station. People were running out and the scene was chaotic. A member of staff directed us to use the stairs as it would be quicker and Andy and I ran down. The staff member shouted from behind us, 'He's covered everything in lighter fluid!' Shit on a stick, this was getting worse.

As we were running down the spiral staircase, people were

running past us in the other direction. They were saying things to us like 'He's fucking mental' and 'He's smashing the place up!' This was getting crazy. I started wondering what I could do with this man to stop him. Andy and I took our batons out: it's better to be safe than sorry.

I'm not sure how long I blacked out for. It could have only been a couple of seconds, because I was still running when I pulled myself together again. But speeding down those spiral stairs had brought on one of my flashbacks. It was a trigger that sent my mind into turmoil and I had no choice in the matter. I was there again, with Gary and the Governor, running down the stairs at Russell Square with the smell of that awful smoke in my nose. It seemed so very real, it was like being in two places and two times all at once.

It is difficult to describe what these episodes were like. I was back in that place in my mind, but I still had rational thoughts about the situation that I was in at the time. I couldn't control what I did in these waking dreams, that was always the same, I could think about doing different things. It just didn't happen. Some were worse than others, like the one I got in my front room on the 21st. But others, like the one I was having this time, I could snap myself out of, if I really focused. All I had to do was shut my eyes and try to concentrate on something good and totally unrelated.

Usually in those situations, I would think of my son. Most of the happy memories from my life centre on him. My favourite image to use was him in his bouncer, which was suspended from a door frame. He used to love being in there and it was easy to think of him bouncing up down, giggling

n manoeuvres on Salisbury Plain on 11 September 2001 I realised that my chances
being deployed to the front line in a war on terror had gone through the roof.
ho knew that my decision that day to leave the army would lead me to experience
rrorism first-hand?

p left: In the Brecon Beacons in 2001 just before I left the army to join the police.

p right: Belize, 1999. An experience of a lifetime when life was a lot simpler, pictured
re during an R&R period while I was on a training exercise.

low: With the lads in Bosnia, 2001. I left home six days after my son was born and
s away for six months.

Top left: My mum behind the bar of her pub in Whitstable.

Top right: Young and skinny. My wedding day, May 1999.

Bottom left: Me and Flo.

© Claire Sawford

Bottom right: Daddy's boy. Brook aged 4.

op: A stretch of water on the Tryweryn River at the Canolfan Tryweryn National Whitewater Centre in Bala, Wales, where two of the bombers who carried out the attacks had gone white-water rafting in June 2005. Remarkably, I was in the area on holiday at the same time.

© *PA Photos*

ottom left: On the top of Mount Snowdon in June 2005.

ottom right: With my mate Gabbi at the summit.

Top: The chillingly familiar image taken from CCTV footage of the four bombers entering Luton station on their way to London.

© Metropolitan Police/Getty Images

Centre left: The tube carriage at Edgware Road. *© PA Photos*

Cente right: The devastating scene I saw inside the tube carriage at Russell Square. *© PA Photos*

Bottom right: As I made my way down the stairs to the Piccadilly Line platform at Russell Square, I heard another explosion, assuming it had come from the tunnel. Little did we know that a bus had exploded above us in nearby Tavistock Square.

© PA Photos

Top: The front pages of the national newspapers on 8 July 2005. © *PA Photos*

Above left: Tributes to the victims of the London bombings started to pile up at Kings Cross as soon as the station reopened. © *PA Photos*

Above right: The Remembrance Plaque at Russell Square. © *PA Photos*

Left: At the remembrance service in St Paul's Cathedral to commemorate those who lost their lives that awful day. I can't think of a more fitting venue, and found it a very sobering experience. © *Getty Images*

Top: Once I knew that Gill had survived, the thought of meeting her again after going through so much together made me incredibly nervous. This is a shot from when we were reunited by the BBC programme, *The Day the Bombs Came*. © B*

Bottom left: Happier times. At Gill's wedding in December 2005. © *Andrew Cro*

Bottom right: Gill and I are still close and see each other regularly. © *Claire Sawfo*

BRITISH TRANSPORT POLICE

The Chief Constable has

COMMENDED

Police Constable 4514 Aaron Debnam

On Thursday, 7th July 2005, London's transport system was the target of a terrorist bombing campaign which resulted in three London Underground trains and one bus being wrecked by explosions, causing the loss of fifty-two innocent lives.

PC Debnam is commended for his outstanding actions at Russell Square Underground Station where, as one of the officers first on scene, he and his colleagues went to the bomb-damaged train and, amidst horrific conditions, assisted with the evacuation of injured passengers.

Chief Constable

EⅡR

The Master of the Household
has received Her Majesty's command to invite

Mr. Aaron Debnam

to a Reception to be given at Buckingham Palace
by The Queen and The Duke of Edinburgh
on Wednesday, 15th February, 2006 at 6.00 p.m.
to mark the work of those involved in
the emergency services and disaster response

A reply is requested to:
The Master of the Household,
Buckingham Palace,
London SW1A 1AA.

Dress: Lounge Suit Day Dress
Uniform Optional

Guests are asked to arrive at Buckingham Palace between 5.15 and 5.50 p.m.

Top: At the British Transport Police commendation ceremony with my chief constable and Alistair Darling MP.

Above: My invitation to Buckingham Palace the day Glen received his MBE.

Left: My Police Commendation certificate for the work I did on 7 July 2005. It took me many months to accept praise and recognition from others just for doing my job.

Evening Standard

LONDON, TUESDAY, 6 SEPTEMBER 2005 · www.thisislondon.co.uk · Incorporating THE EVENING NEWS · 40p

Our biggest restaurant offer ever
Dine from £10pp PAGES 44 & 45

DON'T MISS **ALLISON PEARSON**
COLUMN: PAGE 15

WIN Ashes tickets to the Oval
SPORT: PAGE 61

CS GAS DRAMA ON TUBE TRAIN

Police use spray to overpower man on hammer rampage

BY BO WILSON AND JUSTIN DAVENPORT

THIS is the moment police officers used CS gas to overpower a man running amok on a Tube train.

Commuters fled as the hammer-wielding man began smashing up carriages. Then, brandishing a container of lighter fuel, he threatened to set the whole train alight. The incident happened amid unprecedented security on the Underground in the wake of the suicide bomb attacks.

Passenger Wasim Maqsood said: "I suddenly heard someone shouting to get off the train. I saw people running in panic and heard loud banging sounds.

"I got off my carriage and went to see what was going on. There was a man with a hammer in his hand and ing loudly.

"He was very aggressive and he tr "When everyone was off the trai driver shut all the doors so that the couldn't escape... that's when he s hitting the windows and sma everything. I think people were

Continued on Page

It's satisfying to be reminded that sometimes you can make a difference.

and trying to grab you as you walked past. I would concentrate on this image, and if I was lucky all the bad images went away. I shut it all away back into that dark corner and forgot – for a short while, anyway.

We arrived on the platform just in time to see one of the train windows explode out on to the floor. It sounded like a shotgun blast and the glass travelled the width of the platform. A staff member was standing a safe distance away and told us that the power was off and the trouble-maker in question was stuck on the train. This was a good thing – because he couldn't escape – but also incredibly bad – because we couldn't get to him either.

I could see the man now. He was walking up the train, smashing away with his hammer. But he had something else in his other hand that I couldn't see. Was it a lighter? We had been told that he had sprayed lighter fluid everywhere. We needed to act.

I stepped out where he could clearly see me by one of the smashed windows and said, 'Police! Put your weapon down, put down whatever else is in your hands, put your hands on your head and get on your knees.'

He was only about ten feet away from me at this point; the only thing separating us was the side of the train. When he looked at me, I could see by his eyes that this man was not on the same planet as me. I wasn't going to warn him again, it was pointless.

Dropping my baton on the floor, I drew my CS spray. I took a quick aim and sprayed him in the face. Fuck it, I couldn't afford to take chances with this bloke.

The guy was wearing glasses, and after I finished giving him the normal dosage of CS it didn't affect him. So I emptied the canister on him. I was expecting at least a cry of pain, but I got nothing. The man simply sat down on the bench seat, put his hands in his lap, and closed his eyes. But at least he was not ranting and swinging his hammer any more.

I shouted at the staff member to restore the power – we needed to get on there quickly, as he still had the offending articles in his hands. I wanted this bloke taken out and in cuffs as soon as possible. We still didn't know if he had sprayed lighter fluid everywhere.

A couple of other officers had turned up by now. When we had first arrived on the scene, Andy had tried to call for assistance on our underground radios, but he could not get through. Being the quick thinker that Andy is, he had pressed the panic button on the set and that had brought the whole of London running to our assistance.

The staff member gave us the thumbs-up about the power and said that he would open the door when we wanted. I positioned officers at both sets of doors in the carriage so that the guy could not escape. On my signal, the doors were opened.

We all rushed on at the same time and jumped on the bloke. I wrenched the hammer out of his hand and threw it away, but I couldn't find anything in his other hand. Had I been seeing things? We quickly cuffed him behind his back and kept him on the floor while we did a quick search of the train. I recovered the hammer and placed it in an evidence bag, but I still could not see any lighter.

Then I found his bag. It was close to where he had been

standing when I first saw him. Inside was a half-empty bottle of methylated spirits. God only knows what he was planning to do with it.

That was it – job done, I was pleased with myself. Andy and I had arrived and dealt with the situation within about thirty seconds. The only hold up that we had was waiting for the power to be turned back on.

Andy and I picked the bloke up and led him off the train towards the lifts. We needed to get out of there sharpish, as we were all starting to feel the effects of the gas that I had discharged. If you use CS spray in a confined space, everybody gets some. I have had a lot of exposure to CS gas in the past. The army use it for training purposes, but no matter how much of the stuff you have come into contact with, it never gets any more pleasant.

As we were approaching the lifts, one of our public-order units came running down the stairs to join us. They were dressed in full riot gear, which I thought was a little over the top – Andy and I were only wearing shirts. The sergeant in charge of these officers said to me, 'Where is he?' I replied, 'I take it you are referring to this guy in handcuffs that I am holding covered in CS spray?' I didn't even wait for his reply; I just got in the lift with my prisoner.

When we got outside, the whole world and his wife had turned up, I hadn't seen so many police vehicles since the bombs. It was a nice feeling, though, to know that we had all this support at a touch of a button. But it was an even better feeling to know that Andy and I had it all wrapped up before they even arrived.

The man, who was disturbingly quiet at this stage, was placed in the back of a van that had turned up and was taken away to the police station. Andy and I walked around in the fresh air trying to compose ourselves and get rid of the effects of the CS spray. Everyone there wanted to know what had happened and those that did were walking up to us and patting us on the back. It was a good feeling.

After we had sorted ourselves out a bit, Andy and I went back to the car, which was parked half on, half off the pavement and sticking out into the road with the lights still flashing. We got in and I let out a huge sigh. I was calming down now, but the adrenaline was still coursing through my body and my hands were shaking, I needed a minute before I started driving again. Then Andy said something that I will always remember and always feel proud of when I think of it: 'It is nice to work with someone that I can trust, mate.' That was it, but that small sentence meant more to me than all the praise that I could have had from anyone. 'Same here, mate.' I replied. We were fucking top cops!

That was it, incident over, just another job done and another figure for the force bean-counters. I got the piss taken out of me a little for contaminating nearly a whole Tube station and everybody in it with CS spray, but apart from that it would have been forgotten.

The most important thing to me was that I had had my first real test since the bombings. I had been faced with a highly stressful and potentially dangerous situation and I had handled it right. I had acted without hesitation and I had acted well; I felt proud of myself and more than a little relieved. For that moment in my life it was like I had never been aboard a bomb-damaged train. It was just me, my mate Andy and a hammer-wielding nutcase.

A couple of weeks later, I was sitting on the train on my way into work when my friend Wayne phoned me. I picked up and said hello and Wayne informed me, 'You are on the front cover of the *Evening Standard*!' the first thing I thought was that I had been snapped doing something that I shouldn't have been, like having a sneaky cigarette round the back of a Tube station or something. My heart sank, I was going to get the sack.

But then he said that it was a massive full-page picture of me, spraying that guy in the face at Holland Park. I couldn't believe it; I couldn't remember any press being there, but it had all happened so quickly. How had this happened? I was very excited, as soon as I got to Victoria I ran to the *Evening Standard* seller and looked at the front page and sure enough, there I was. I bought three copies.

I couldn't have asked for a better photo, I was standing there in exactly the position that I should have been, spraying my CS through the broken window of a train. You could even see the jet of liquid coming out of the nozzle and going into the bloke's face in one continuous stream. I was thrilled – I was famous!

I phoned Andy straight away to tell him. He was in the picture as well, standing directly behind me, with his baton drawn ready to react. The headline at the top read: 'CS GAS DRAMA ON TUBE TRAIN'.

The picture ended up in nearly every Transport Police

station in London as well as the training establishments and for a few weeks I was famous in police circles. But not one of our managers came to me or Andy to say, 'Well done.' Ours is a thankless job sometimes.

Chapter Twenty

THE BBC

Since the time of the bombings, our force press officer had been pestering me and my colleagues about interviews. Requests had come in from all over the place, from all the major networks and papers, for officers to speak to them about the bombings. Mainly I ignored these, but something happened to change my mind.

I was watching the news on TV during a break at work. A woman who had survived the bomb blast at King's Cross was being interviewed. She had not been in the carriage where the bomb went off, but farther down the train, and she was complaining about the emergency response from all the services, how long it took us to reach them in the tunnels and how no one on the day had even thought to take her name.

This woman infuriated me so much that I turned her off. I could not listen to her prattle on about how hard done by she was just because no one paid her much attention on the day. Did she not realise that we had more important things to do than make lists? But the thing that pissed me off the most was the fact that the public were listening to her and some might even take her seriously.

Something needed to be said; someone had to speak for us. No one from any emergency services that attended the scenes had been on the TV yet. There were plenty of interviews with senior officers, but none had been done with those of us that were on the scene. No one knew what we had been through that day and the only thing I was hearing from this woman on the TV was criticism.

About a week before this, I had received an email from our press officer. He was looking for volunteers to do interviews for a documentary that the BBC was making. I had ignored this at first – I wasn't really interested in being on TV, I do not really like being the centre of attention. But this woman on the television inspired me to do it. I needed to have my say.

I asked the other guys on my team if they were interested, but all said that they were not. I tried to persuade them because I did not want to do it on my own, but they would not budge. However, I was determined by now. I wanted to put the public straight; our story needed to be told.

I phoned the press officer to express my interest in the offer and he was back to me within a couple of days. I was to go to the BBC studios in Shepherd's Bush and have a chat with the producer of this programme in a week's time.

After calming down about it a little, however, I started having second thoughts. If I were to be interviewed, I would have to go into a lot of detail about the event. I would have to tell a nation about what I had seen and I would have to try and hide my grief from all those people. It is one thing being weak in front of people you know, but it is a whole different kettle of fish doing it in front of a nation.

I started to practise then. I picked out what events were relevant, and I started to expand on my pre-prepared story that I had been telling to the head-shrinkers. I was not going to get caught out, but I still wanted to get our story across.

When I told the guys at work what I was doing they all took the piss, but I had expected that. It was still only a few weeks after I was in the *Evening Standard* and various jokes were being flung around. People would stop me and ask if they needed to consult my agent before speaking to me; all of it was light-hearted and fun – not enough to put me off doing it.

The week afterwards, I went by train to Shepherd's Bush for my appointment with the BBC. The producer came and met me and we sat outside one of the coffee shops and chatted for a good hour. I gave him my rehearsed sequence of events and he was excited about it. I was the first member of the BTP to come forward to them and they desperately wanted to hear our version of what happened on that day.

A date was set for my interview to take place; it was to be at the London Fire Brigade Headquarters on the south bank of the Thames. They planned to do my interview directly after the chief fire officer. I turned up in good time and had to sit around for a bit. The fact that I knew that I was supposed to talk about it had really stressed me out. It had

got me thinking about the events of the day and all the stuff
that I had tried so hard to bury was seeping out and affecting
me quite badly.

I hadn't slept a wink the night before. I had tossed and
turned all night, worrying about cracking up on camera.
What a stupid bastard I was. I had managed to hide all this
from everyone for a couple of months and now I was going
to tell the nation what I hadn't even told my closest friends.
Half the stuff that I was going to say I had even avoided
thinking about. If my mind had previously wandered on to
it, I used to stuff it back into the deepest recess of my mind.
I was bad. Some of the worst nightmares that I had came in
the week preceding that interview.

It was not long before I was shown into a room and sat in
front of a camera. The room was very dark and there were
four other people in there with me. I was asked to sit still
while they moved the camera about me, for some reason.
The camera was really close to my face and was making me
feel uncomfortable. It was also on a rail that went in a semi-
circle around my right-hand side. One minute it was in my
face, the next it was by my side; it was really hard not to
follow it with my eyes.

The interview started by me giving them an account of
what I had done on the day and where I'd been. It was
basically what I had rehearsed. No problem, I kept it
together. I mentioned Gill, but only the stuff that I had
hardened myself to – nothing more. My account was not
detailed and it steered clear of talking about gory details and
how I felt emotionally.

Then the producer started asking me questions. He obviously had them well thought out, and had them in front of him before I started. He must have based them on the conversation that we'd had the week before. I am sure he did not mean to start stressing me out, but every question attacked what I was trying to hide. I did the best I could to evade the really deep-reaching ones and gave robotic responses, but some of them really hit the spot.

I could feel myself losing it. Most of his questions were about Gill. My eyes were welling up, my heart was pounding and I started to sweat. The deeper he delved, the worse it became. I was starting to react physically again. My chest tightened and I was so very hot. I am sure that I managed to hide it. But all I wanted to do was get out of there.

The end came mercifully quickly. I think that he realised that he wasn't going to get any more out of me than he already had. And I was quite visibly upset by now. I said my goodbyes and ran rather than walked out of the building. Once outside, I smoked a cigarette and calmed myself down, I started to regret the whole interview immediately. I shouldn't have done it, this might have been the first time that I had shown any weakness since the event and I'd done it on television. What a prick.

The people from the BBC were really nice to me. The guy that did the interview could not have known that I harboured so much grief and guilt from the day. He was just doing his job. I regret doing it now as much as ever: it drew attention to me at work that I did not need at the time and now everyone knew how upset I was over the incident, whereas I would have rather they hadn't at the time.

But the BBC was not all a bad experience for me. In fact, they did me the biggest favour that anyone could have – as you'll see later.

Chapter Twenty-One

FINSBURY PARK

As I have said, things were going well for me at work. I was working hard and getting results. The bosses were happy because I was performing and I was happy because I was at work so much that I did not have time to think. I didn't want anything to change.

I was still pretty cut up about things, but I had buried it all so deep that the flashbacks were coming less often than before. And even when they did come, I had managed to find a level on which I could integrate them into my life. I would think about those other things and they would go away. I could function normally outwardly, despite being in total despair inside.

I was also relying heavily on my friends at work. I felt like they were my only support as they were the only ones who could possibly understand what I was feeling. We did not purposely sit down and talk about the events, but we would discuss it most of the time, as events were still quite recent. This was a small but important outlet for me, it was my only vent, and these were the only people that I felt comfortable talking to. But soon I was to lose this support and it hit me hard.

This is the first time that I have ever spoken about it. The guys at work do not realise how important they were to me at the time. We had become closer as a team overnight and as I have already said, friends for life.

Back in April 2005, I had applied for a post as a response driver at a new station that was opening up. The BTP already had foot officers at Finsbury Park, but planned to start up a mobile-response capability from that location to improve response times in the area. I had been toying with the idea of leaving central London for a while before the new jobs were advertised. I had come as far as I could in that location, wanted to get promoted and felt that the best way to do that was to work with new officers who did not know me so well and had not seen my development as an officer from day one.

After a lot of thought, I submitted my application. It was accepted and I was sent on my response-driving course in north Wales quickly afterwards. I was actually looking forward to going. It would be a fresh start, a new area to learn and new people to work with. This was a good move for me, I was sure. But I only felt like this before the events that July.

After the bombings, I was only just coping. As I have said, I was relying on my friends and the familiarity of the area and the people in it was stability that I needed at the time. I did not need any more stress in my life – I had enough to deal with.

I came into work on a Wednesday and looked at the roster that was on the wall to see what I was doing the following week, only to find that my name had been struck off. I knew what this meant immediately and was absolutely gutted. I don't know what I thought would have happen after the bombings, but I guess I thought that the force would see that I needed stability and support and would withdraw my transfer. I had previously expressed a reluctance to go because of the change of circumstances, but was ignored.

According to the roster, I was to report for duty at Finsbury Park on the Sunday. I did not have much time to adjust. I went to see the chief inspector and told him that I did not want to go. I tried to explain the reasons why, but to do this fully I had to let on that I wasn't coping, so I chose not to tell him the whole truth. I tried everything I could think of to avoid going, but the answer was always the same. I was going and there was nothing I could do about it.

I tried to think positively and convince myself that it would be fine and that I would be able to cope without my friends. I even started to look forward to it again as I tried to remind myself of the reasons why I had wanted to go in the first place. But on some level I must have known that I wouldn't have been OK – and I would be proved right.

I started working up at Finsbury on the Sunday; it was a settling-in shift for me. I had to move all my kit into my new locker, meet my new shift mates and generally learn how things operated at this new station. It was a much smaller place than the one I had come from, with a lot less people, and was next to Finsbury Park Tube and bus station. The station was a depressing place, so very grey and dull. It felt like a prison inside, with small, high windows and bare, plain walls. Because there were not as many people there as I was used to, it seemed very empty and cold. I didn't like it from the start.

The officers on my new team seemed like a nice bunch. They were all quite young in service and relatively inexperienced, as they had only ever been foot officers working a very limited mandate. They had not had the benefit of being mobile and attending a whole range of incidents, which is the quickest way to gain experience.

There were only four of us on the team and I was the senior PC. This was what I had come to this place for, to gain experience leading others. I was not their superior in any sense of the word, but being more experienced I had hoped that I could help the others, guide them as best I could and give them advice. It would be a step in the right direction on the career path.

Things went OK for the first week or so, I was still settling in and getting to know the area, and this kept me amused for the time being. I still didn't have time to think. But this could not last too long. There was one overriding problem with my new posting and that was that it was not busy. I couldn't believe how dead it was. This was north London; it was supposed to be the Wild West. But no, I was taking crap calls and dealing with ticket touts and beggars. Don't get me wrong, these people have to be dealt with as well, but when it is all you're doing it is soul destroying.

This was not good for me, not in the state that I was in. I needed to be active the whole time. I could not be dealing with all this low-level stuff that I could do with my eyes shut. I needed excitement, I needed to be whizzing around on the blue lights, I needed my friends, I needed to be doing anything but this.

All the images and emotions that I had tried so hard to suppress were starting to leak out. I had stopped sleeping and was grumpy all the time. My mood swings were huge and I had no control over them at all. One minute I would be super happy, the next I would be snappy and irritable with those around me. I did not know what to feel or how to cope. I had no one to talk to, these new people couldn't possibly understand how I felt; I was coming apart. The fragile little bubble that I had built for myself was breaking after just a couple of weeks.

At the time, I thought I was trying to fix the problem, to find a happy medium, a place where I could operate normally and hide all of these negative feelings. I was still working the same hours as Gary and the others, so I was finding any excuse to drive down and see them. Just for a quick chat, a smoke and a coffee. But it wasn't enough, not by a long way. The cracks were opening wider and I was falling to pieces.

In early September, three weeks after getting to Finsbury Park, I called in sick. I got out of bed one morning after another horrible night and I just couldn't face it. I needed to sort myself out; I needed to be able to sleep, at least.

I spoke to my GP and got some sleeping pills from him, I also spoke to the Occupational Health team at work and arranged to go and see them. I was still adamant that I could sort my own head out: all I needed was a break from work and some sleep, then I would be fine again.

I had a good chat with the Occupational Health team, admitting that my problems and lack of sleep were related to what I had been through during the bombings, but without going into any detail. They offered me a counselling service, an independent woman who specialises in working with victims of trauma. 'Why not,' I thought. At least it was confidential – no one that I knew would have to hear about what was going on in my head. So I took it. I didn't think that I particularly needed any help, but anything was worth a try.

I had nine sessions with this woman and although she was really nice, it was the biggest waste of time imaginable for me. All I did was sit in a small room and chat. We hardly ever talked about my trauma; it was just general chit-chat about relationships and everyday life. If the conversation did drift on to the subject of my trauma, my defences would go up, but she didn't even try to get around them. She never pushed me, she never tried to force me and as lovely as she was, she certainly didn't help me.

Looking back now, I think I was there for a reason. This was the first time that I had accepted any help. I was still certain at the time that I didn't need any, but I had put myself in a position where I could be. This was the first step that I had taken towards getting better, and it hadn't worked. It put me off the idea completely. This woman was a professional and – to my way of thinking back then – she hadn't fixed me. It was clear to me that I was going to have to carry on and hope that things sort themselves out.

I went back to work after two weeks. The sleeping pills had been knocking me out for the count, the break from work had done me good and I was feeling rested. I had been talking on the phone with Gary and the others and had even met them for drinks a couple of times in London. But something else had made me feel good. Something had happened to me while I was off that made me feel a whole lot better. I was about to meet someone who would change my whole outlook on life.

Chapter Twenty-Two

ALIVE

It was just another day for me. I was sitting in the pub on some random weekday having a pint and doing the crossword. It's hard sometimes doing shifts: when you are off during the week all your mates are at work and you are left with nothing to do but kill time until they finish.

Anyway, so there I was, stuck on a clue but not really that bothered about the answer, when my phone rang. I remember the conversation like it was yesterday. It was the producer from the documentary that I had done with the BBC and he told me something that at first I didn't believe. I was shocked into silence. I hardly spoke on the phone, I simply listened. I just about managed to say goodbye to the bloke and agree to what he had suggested we do next. When I put my phone back down on the bar, I simply stared into space.

At first I was speaking to myself. I can't even remember

who was in the pub at the time, they must have thought I was mental! 'She's alive,' I said, quietly at first. 'I can't believe it, she's alive!' came next a little louder. With that I left my pint and ran to my mate's shop. I needed internet access and I needed it now.

I ran into the shop and said to my mate Paul, 'She's alive, dude, I need to use your computer!' The poor guy must have seen the look on my face, because although he looked puzzled, he agreed at once. I went online and accessed one of the major daily paper's websites – and there she was. Gill was alive, she had given an interview for this paper, and she was ALIVE!

There was a photo on the web page and there she was, the woman that I had carried out of that train, the woman that I had thought was dead for over two months, – alive! I was all over the place; I couldn't take this information in. I could see it right there on the screen in front of me, but still it did not seem real.

I am in tears writing this. I can't describe the emotions that I felt at the time – it was all the good ones. I was happy, relieved, proud, excited, but most of all I was at peace – for the moment, at least.

I suppose I'd better fill you in on the phone conversation that I had before I continue – it becomes relevant later. Basically, the guy from the BBC had told me that Gill was alive, he had seen the article in the paper and passed the information on to me. He also mentioned that they were trying to contact her and they were going to ask if she would do an interview for them for the documentary they were making. But the best bit was that they were going to ask her if she would like to meet me and another officer who was on the documentary with me. I was well up for this, I can tell you. Wild fucking horses wouldn't have kept me away from that woman. I wanted to tell her everything. I wanted to tell her how much her life meant to me, I wanted to give her a big hug and just say, 'Thank you for being alive, and I think you have saved me from myself.'

I'm crying again, as I write this. I'm going for a smoke…

That's better!

I was on cloud nine that day. When I think back, it was the first day since the bombings that I hadn't experienced any flashbacks or mood swings. I still didn't sleep that night, but it was out of excitement more than anything else. I phoned Gary, Chris, and Ray. I told my mum, all of my mates. I would have told the world if I could have. SHE WAS ALIVE! I had the spring back in my step.

The next couple of days were like a dream. I was checking my phone constantly. The guy from the BBC had said that he would phone me when they had managed to contact her and tell me if she had agreed to meet me. The wait was awful. When he did eventually ring, about a week later, the news was good.

Apparently, she had jumped at the chance and we were to meet in Richmond in early October. This was a little over two weeks away, I think, and I was nervous from the outset. What would I say to this woman? What would she be like? Would she remember me? And the strangest thing of all: would she blame me for hurting her? After all, she had screamed when I picked her up and put her on my shoulder. Would she judge me for the amount of time we took to get to her? Would she blame me for the amount of time we took to get her out? This doesn't make sense to me now, but at the time my mind and my train of thought were not exactly the epitome of rationality.

When I had read the newspaper interview that Gill had done, it brought a little realism to the injuries that she had sustained. Before, she had just been the woman that had died; now she was very much alive and was having to live with the horrible wounds. I kept thinking that the woman must be going through hell. All I had to remember her by were my memories from the tunnel. I half expected to see her in Richmond covered in black soot wearing a filthy white T-shirt and a blood-stained pair of jeans.

Although I was overjoyed at finding out that Gill had survived, my good mood did not last long. Negative thoughts almost immediately began festering in my mind, and in turn they made way for the return of my nightmares. In short, the good news had ultimately made no real difference to the way that I was feeling. I couldn't understand it. Gill was alive, why was I still feeling guilty when I was thinking and dreaming about her in that tunnel? I couldn't understand it, all that negative emotion should be gone by now. When I thought about Gill rationally it was OK, but as soon as I thought about her in relation to the incident, the bad feelings came back. Whenever I thought of her in that tunnel, or of leaving her in the booking hall, I felt exactly as I had on the day itself.

Chapter Twenty-Three

TREADING WATER

Back at work, things were going from bad to worse. Because I did not know anybody well in the station when I arrived, no one could have known the person that I was before. As a result, no one could see the change in me. I had gone from being a keen, capable officer to a moody, ignorant, solitary person at work who people were wary of being around. I honestly think that if I had stayed at my old station then the people that knew me best at work would have noticed the change and I would have got help sooner than I did.

The other four officers on my team were good people, but it did not take them long to learn to keep me at arm's length. You could just never tell what mood I would come into work with. One day I would be my old self, happy, bubbly and a bit of a clown. The next, I would storm into the station with a face like thunder and people would obviously avoid me when this was the case. I was overcritical of the actions of the other officers I worked with and when we went to an incident I would handle it like they were not even there. I would work on my own whenever possible and nine times out of ten when this was the case I would go back to my old station as often as I could. Just seeing my old friends and chatting with them would make me feel better.

Night shifts were the worst. It would only be the three of us in the station and I got bored easily. I would spend hours out in the yard, smoking and lost in my own thoughts. No prizes for guessing what I was thinking about. I was my own worst enemy, but I couldn't see it. I had come to hate the place that I worked and was slowly starting to hate my job; I had never thought this would happen. For the past two and a half years, the job had been my life. I was the only person that I knew who used to look forward to coming to work.

In short, I had had enough of Finsbury Park and wanted to go back to my old station. I sat at my computer one afternoon and typed a formal request to go back and sent it to the station inspector. I couldn't stay there any more; I was coming apart at the seams. The station inspector was fair with me, but it was clear that he was not going to let me go without a fight. He said that he would consider my request after three months. If I still felt the same after that, then he would send it up the chain of command to be considered. This seemed like the best offer I was going to get, so I agreed, but at the same time I was sure that I would be counting down the days.

Chapter Twenty-Four

REUNIONS

The day had finally come when I was to meet Gill. I can't even begin to tell you how nervous I was. I had taken extra-special care preparing my uniform that morning, I had shaved (a rarity, even now) and I had done my hair. It was like going on a date dressed as a copper.

The meeting was in Richmond Town Hall and I had no idea what to expect. The plan was that I would be picked up by a driver at work and driven from north London to Richmond in the south. I thought this very cool. The Tube journey to Richmond is a nightmare and being driven down there was my idea of luxury.

I was picked up from the bus station outside and it took us well over an hour to get through the late-afternoon London traffic. I had more time than I needed to have a good think – and worry more – about meeting this woman.

I had been a complete nervous wreck for the days immediately beforehand; I must have been a nightmare to be around. I was very excited about meeting her, but at the same time I was petrified.

I have already mentioned that my episodes were brought on by triggers; this woman was the biggest trigger of them all. What if I started to wig out in front of her? I was turning myself into a right old state. By the time we arrived in Richmond, I didn't even want to get out of the car. I had seriously considered asking the driver to drop me off at the Tube station, but I couldn't back out of this now.

As I walked up the driveway of the place where we were to meet Gill, I was greeted by a whole host of different people from the BBC along with the other officer who was on the documentary with me. I was really nervous and just wanted to get it over with, but the BBC wanted photos and footage of us walking into the building. This is when I first became suspicious of the circumstances under which I was to meet Gill.

I think that it was the council offices where the meeting was due to take place. It was quite a grand building, set in lovely grounds. You walked in through a large pair of iron gates and up a long gravel driveway towards the house. I do not think that the house was actually that old, but it certainly looked the part. I felt that I should have been arriving in a horse-drawn carriage rather than by diesel saloon car.

I was under the impression that it was to be a very low-key affair and that they would let us meet first and then do the interviews later, but this was not the case. I was to walk into a room and meet Gill while being filmed. I was so uncomfortable with this that initially I refused. I couldn't do what they were asking of me. I was already so worried about not being able to handle the situation and breaking down, I couldn't face running the risk of doing it and having it immortalised on film.

After expressing my concerns to the BBC, I went and sat on a bench seat in the lobby of the building that we were in, quite contented to let the other officer go in on his own and for me to meet Gill after the fanfare was over. Then a woman came and sat next to me, I'm still not entirely sure who she was, but she started talking me into it. She was a very persuasive person and told me that it was important for this part of the story to be captured on film. Something about emotional impact was also mentioned, but she had already swayed me by that point.

So it was that I found myself standing in front of the door to this room, wondering what I would find on the other side. The other officer that I was with stood in front of me and didn't really look fazed about anything. I was more than happy with him going in first; I had planned to hang around by the door and assess the situation in the room before I committed myself anyway. If it looked dodgy, then I was going to walk right out of the building. This may sound a bit cowardly, but I was looking after number one at this point. I was not going to make a fool of myself on national TV.

The door opened and there she was – STANDING! I remembered her immediately and was dumb-struck. I just stood there in the door like a lemon. I didn't even notice the cameras, all my focus was on her. She was propped up on crutches and was smiling at us. I looked at her face and could remember every feature. I looked at her hands and could remember holding them in that dreadful tunnel. This was the woman who I had grieved so much for and now she was here in the flesh.

I could tell by the way that she was leaning heavily on the crutches that she had not been on her new legs for long. She was kind of stooped over and I could see the strain that her body weight was putting on her hands. I was still amazed, though – she was standing on prosthetic limbs after only two and a half months. I was visualising the injuries that she had sustained and I couldn't believe it. She had lost both legs below the knee, she had the inside of one of her thighs blown off, and she had sustained a horrible injury to her back that was caused by the piece of human shrapnel. This truly was an amazing woman.

The room was quite bare as far as furniture was concerned. I think there was a small table up against one of the walls and there were a few chairs off to the left. It was very bright in there, the windows were massive and the early winter sun was pouring through them on to the walls. The main thing that filled the room was the equipment that the BBC was using. I think that there were several cameras in there, plus all the sound-recording equipment and also things whose function was a mystery to me. All this and the blandness of the room made me feel like I was walking into a laboratory and that I was a test subject.

The other officer walked over and hugged Gill and still I

stood there staring. She hugged him back and I was still motionless. When he was done hugging she looked directly at me and I knew those eyes. She beckoned me over with those eyes and the trance was broken.

I hugged her, tentatively at first, like you would hug a friend or an aunty, but she drew me in. I felt a huge release of emotion and I let go. I hugged her back and I felt her bury her face in my neck. It was all I could do to fight off the tears that were brimming in my eyes. I knew this woman. I knew her better than I knew myself. I had shared an experience with her that so few know. I, and the others with me, had carried her life in our hands. I had shed blood, sweat and tears for her. I would have given my life in her place on the day and now here she was in my arms, in an embrace that seemed to last for an eternity.

She was tiny. I could have wrapped my arms around her twice. I didn't think I could ever let her go. She had been dead to me for two months. Her face had haunted my waking dreams and my nightmares. Her blood had soaked my clothes and her life had been the most important thing to me all that way under the ground. But she was here and I loved her.

Eventually I let her go. I kissed her on the cheek and walked away to where I assumed we were supposed to sit. Something had passed between us in that embrace, something that to this day neither I nor she can put into words, but I knew at that moment in time when I was holding her that I would know this woman for the rest of my life.

I sat in a daze. At some point everyone else sat and began to talk. Gill was trying to thank us, but it wasn't right. I tried to speak to her but it was all wrong. I looked at the cameras and just said, 'That's enough, can you leave us?' There was no protest, they just left all their equipment and left the room. It was just the three of us, and then Gill's fiancé Joe joined us too.

We chatted and talked about our experiences, drank tea and chatted some more. It felt quite strained. I didn't know what to say to this woman. I had all the emotions in me that I have just spoken about and I wanted to tell her everything. But I didn't, I sat there like a shy schoolboy and just chatted, when I really wanted to say more. Every time our eyes met I would look away – I didn't want to feel them probing into my soul again. Those eyes opened wounds. They dug away at all the stuff that I had buried. There was nothing but care and love in her eyes but they were exposing my weaknesses and I couldn't allow that to happen.

We sat in that room for a little over three-quarters of an hour and I felt very uncomfortable for the whole time. I was constantly holding back my emotions and every now and again I would get very hot and start to smell smoke, but I squashed it back down. I felt like the little Dutch boy with his finger in a dam. I didn't have a clue what to say to this woman. She had been the centre of all my feelings surrounding that day and now I was sitting in a room drinking tea out of a bone-china cup with her. Every time I looked at her face I could see her in that stretcher covered with black soot, staring blankly at the ceiling of the tunnel. I wanted to touch her hand to see if it was still as cold as ice.

When the meeting was over it was a relief. The crew from the BBC came in and the tension that I felt was broken. They started to fuss around us and make arrangements for us to be driven back to our homes by the cars that had brought us to the meeting. All the time, I could feel this woman looking at me; it felt like she wanted more from me somehow, like she wanted to know my thoughts. I was scared of her. I was petrified that she saw through the barriers that I had built up in the previous months.

We all left the building together and walked out on to the large gravel driveway. I had come to the conclusion that I had done my part now, it was over for me, and it was time to put that day in the past. I had to move on with my life and part of that was not to see this woman again. I knew that if I saw her then it would open the wounds that I had tried so hard to close over. I had met her now and that was it. I knew she was alive and that was all I needed to get over my guilt. I would go home, go to bed and tomorrow was the first day of the rest of my life. Sorted, I had my head screwed on; I knew what I was doing. I wasn't running away, I was giving myself space.

I was quite pleased with myself thinking this – it sounded like a positive move. I had no reason to see this woman again now. It was all finished for me. Then Joe walked up to me and said something to me that would ruin all of this: 'Gill and I are getting married soon, we would like it very much if you could come.' SHIT, what did he have to go and say that for? I was moving on and now I'm back to square one. I smiled, though, and accepted the invitation. What else could I do? Talk about being on the spot.

When the cars finally turned up, I gave Gill one last painful hug and said my goodbyes. I jumped in the silver Mercedes and couldn't resist saying 'Home, James' to the driver. All the way back to my home in Kent, my mind was not in that car. The driver must have thought me a right arrogant git; I hardly said a word to him. I was lost in thought all the way home. I was thinking about how that woman made me feel and how I had nearly broken down when I was with her. I was thinking about all the feelings and emotions that she stirred up in me, but most of all I was thinking about how she reminded me so completely of that day. I could think of nothing else when I was around her. It was all we had talked about and it had started to chip away at my walls. I couldn't expose myself to that again. There was no way that I was going to that wedding. I had made my decision and that was final.

Besides, it couldn't be healthy having any type of relationship with her, could it? I mean, I was involved in her rescue but that didn't mean that I had to know this woman afterwards, did it? I was just doing my job wasn't I? Firemen don't have relationships with every life that they save; neither do paramedics, doctors or nurses. I had just been involved with saving one life when people from the other professions I have just mentioned probably saved dozens. I had talked myself into it. I wasn't going to see this woman again.

On the way home, my phone rang. I looked at the display and it was a text from Gill. We had exchanged numbers in Richmond, but I hadn't expected to hear from her so soon. The text said something like, 'Great to see you, I hope that you can make it to the wedding.' I replied, but I still did not plan to go. I thought that if I kept my distance then she would forget and I could get on with mending my head on my own.

Writing this chapter really slammed home for me how messed up I was at the time and how much emotion I had buried in my head. I could almost feel the same as I had on the day and as I remembered I have cried more than once. It had been amazing to see Gill on that day, to see her standing had been both unexpected and breathtaking; she truly is an amazing woman. But at that instant when I held her in my arms, I felt such a rush of emotion and I simply couldn't deal with it at the time. I had spent so long suppressing what I felt and now all this woman had to do was look at me and I could feel it flooding out. I had thought at the time that the simplest solution was to avoid her at all costs – that would be the safe option. But I know now that I couldn't have been more wrong.

Chapter Twenty-Five

SYMPTOMS

The emotions that I felt after my meeting with Gill were just as strong as they were before I found out that she was alive. Even the guilt about failing to save her life was still present, although I couldn't understand it at the time. I knew she was alive, I had seen her, spoken to her and touched her, but my feelings had not changed. It is only now that I know about my condition that I can explain such a bizarre contradiction properly.

At this point, it feels appropriate to tell you a little bit about post-traumatic stress disorder, or PTSD for short. I have touched on this briefly before, but you need to know a little more about it before we continue.

When the human brain struggles to take in and process all the information that it takes in during a traumatic event, it is forced to store it in a job lot. Everything from physical

169

feelings to the images that you see, even the emotions that you feel at the time, is stored together as a mixed-up mess of memories. As I have already said, PTSD sufferers experience flashbacks and bad dreams, as it is the mind's way of trying to process that information, but as well as physical reactions and vivid images in your head, you also suffer the same emotions that you were feeling at the time.

This is because the brain has stored all these things together. It is like the nasty version of seeing something that you enjoy and smiling because your brain associates that thing with being happy. That is a trigger, but a trigger for me would bring a rush of negative feelings and horrible physical reactions.

Whenever I saw a Tube tunnel my pulse would quicken and I'd be on high alert. Whenever I smelt smoke I would find it difficult to breath and I would get very hot, and when I saw Gill I would feel incredibly guilty and inadequate. I think that you have to experience it to properly understand it. It doesn't make a whole lot of sense, but you have to believe that it is totally involuntary, the sufferer simply has no choice in what they feel at the time. The worst bit of it is that if you don't deal with what is going on in your head at the time, then you end up suffering for a lot longer.

It is a very confusing time: you know what you should be feeling, but you feel something completely different. Sometimes you feel right about something – my feelings towards Gill were normal on occasion. But I couldn't trust them; I didn't know what my reaction around Gill was going to be because I was so unstable. I would be standing with this woman, she would be close enough to touch, but I would still be feeling guilty about not being able to save her life.

She took me back to that place and that time. I would see her face and be transported back to that tunnel. I would be having a conversation with her about the weather and at the same time I would be holding her hand and checking her pulse in my mind. It was like living two realities simultaneously. It is so difficult to describe. She was the centre of my world that day and now she was the centre of my pain, the catalyst of my feelings and the most important person in my life at the time. Now, if that isn't confusing, then I don't know what is.

By this stage, I had gone into a symptomatic stage called 'avoidance'. My grief was so deeply buried that I needed to avoid things that reminded me of it. Things like the Tube, the news and certain things at work, I was starting to get used to and to deal with. I wasn't getting the same reaction from them as I was in the beginning. But Gill was a completely different ball game. She was a double-edged sword: she could make me feel wonderful and proud, but at the same time she could make me feel like my world was crumbling down around my shoulders. She was my biggest trigger and to avoid feeling bad, I had convinced myself that I should stay away from her. To avoid Gill would avoid having to deal with my problems.

Another symptom, and one that I was suffering from quite badly, was the feeling of isolation. This was particularly apparent at Finsbury Park. I felt like no one understood what I was going through, that no one understood me at all. I had not felt so isolated at my previous station because I had Gary and the others to lean on. But now I felt so alone, with no one to express myself to. Even at home, as supportive as my friends and family were at the time, I still felt very alone. I could be sitting in a pub full of people and still be lonely. I would be lost in my thoughts and I knew that I could not relate to any of these people around me. None of them would have had the same experiences as me and I would suffer in silence.

I think about my own personal circumstances sometimes and ask: why? Why did that event effect me so severely when I have seen so much in my life? This was not my first major incident – I had been to well over a dozen fatalities before this, and I had never had a problem before. The worst thing that had happened to me before was seeing the bodies of young children after a major train wreck, but I had coped with that. Why now? Why this?

What I had seen may have been horrific, but on the scale of things that have happened in history the loss of life was not that great. I had known people in the army who had witnessed genocide first hand in Rwanda, people who had seen their friends blown up by roadside bombs in Ireland and people who had been to Bosnia and Kosovo at the height of those conflicts. Admittedly, some of these had been affected, but not at all. Whenever I think about horrific events, I think about D Day and the extermination of the Jews during the Second World War. Millions of people were involved in these events and survived. Were they all suffering from PTSD?

All this has led me to believe that we all have things in our subconscious that help us cope with traumatic events. Our brains protect themselves by shielding out what they cannot deal with. But if you are exposed to an event so horrific when you are at a heightened state of awareness, then your brain shrugs off those protection systems and soaks it all up. I have been told since the event that my claustrophobia may have been the main cause of my PTSD: because my brain was already on a heightened state of alert when I was faced with the prospect of entering the tunnel, when I arrived at the scene it just absorbed everything that it could. I suffered from traumatic information overload and my mind could not take the pressure.

PTSD normally takes hold when a person is faced by his or her death. Earlier, I alluded to all the worries that we had when first entering the tunnel – secondary explosions, fire and tunnel collapse. I had blanked all of these out, suppressed them before I started down the tunnel, but they were still probably present in my subconscious. I was petrified of that tunnel collapsing, worst of all because of my claustrophobia, so even though I didn't feel scared at the time, who is to say that, in the far reaches of my mind, I wasn't scared of dying. I certainly think that this is the case with me.

I have already mentioned that I started to remember things after the event that had happened but for some reason I had blanked them out. When this was happening, it felt like complete torture. Just when you think that you have enough terrible images and memories in your head, you remember another. I can't convey how upsetting this is. I would find myself drifting off in to a dream world and when I came back to reality I would have remembered something that I had completely suppressed. I would only have to see something that my brain associated with that memory or that image and it would happen exactly the same as if I was reliving the other events.

I think that the worse one came when I was sitting with Gill in her front room one day. I had popped up to see her after I had finished work and we were just chatting over one of her amazing coffees. She mentioned something about the bombings and the other lads who had worked with her that day. We were talking about a conversation she had with a Met copper. He had been discussing how hard it had been to carry her because of her injuries and the fact that we didn't have a stretcher made things a hundred times worse. She told me that this bloke and one other had picked her up by the belt and they had carried her like a hand bag because there was literally no other way they could do it and we had tried everything else. I hadn't even given this a thought since the day. I knew I must have been there because I didn't leave Gill's side until we took her upstairs, but I couldn't remember a thing about it.

Then something clicked. One minute I am sitting in the pleasant surroundings of Gill's flat, the next I am transported a year back in time to that tunnel in the dark. I can see clearly the two officers trying to half-carry, half-drag Gill along holding her belt. I was standing in front of them off to one side with my hands on my knees, struggling with my breath and at the point of giving up. I can even remember what I was thinking: I thought that she

174

had died. She was all limp and there looked to be no life in her whatsoever. She was facing downwards with her hand and what was left of her legs dragging on the floor. I could see the strain in the two officers' faces and felt despair for them as they struggled along.

I am not sure how long I was seeing this image for, but I only noticed that I was staring off into space when I came to with Gill looking at me strangely. This was not the first time that this had happened and it sure as hell would not be the last. I was plagued by events like this for more than a year afterwards. I suppose it was just my brain trying to process the information again, but it was a horrible experience and trying to function normally when these kind of things are going on in your head is nigh-on impossible.

On the whole, I think that a lot of different factors contributed to my condition. It was the trauma equivalent of the planets being re-aligned. I was in the wrong place at the wrong time doing the wrong thing in the worst conditions – like everyone else that day.

PTSD is not an easy thing to talk about. It comes in all different shapes and sizes. Everyone who suffers from it displays roughly the same symptoms, but their conditions have all come about in different ways and for different reasons. Some people may be survivors of a terrorist attack, a plane crash or even an abusive relationship. Everyone is different, but everybody suffers.

Awareness of this condition needs to be raised – not just in the emergency services, but in all walks of life. Take this, for instance. I went to my GP to make him aware of my situation – I had already been diagnosed by a psychiatric nurse but had to see my GP so it went on my records. I sat in that office and told him what the problem was and he asked me to tell him about the condition because he didn't know that much about it. This is all kinds of wrong. What if I had been someone who didn't have support at work available to me? Who would I have turned to with my problems if not my GP? It simply is not good enough. PTSD came within a hair's breadth of ruining my life; I would not have pulled myself away from the edge without the support that I got from specialists. Those people knew what they were talking about and led me through the process by my nose. I was helpless without them.

Line managers and supervisors in high-risk occupations need to learn how to recognise the signs and symptoms of this condition. It should be part of their training. PTSD is not something that sets in overnight; it is something that creeps up on you and takes hold without you realising it. These people need to be able to spot this condition so that it can be addressed at the earliest stage possible. Something needs to be done.

Chapter Twenty-Six

UPHILL
STRUGGLES

I really wish that I could say that things started to get better after I met Gill, but they didn't. If anything, they got worse. I was still at Finsbury Park and I was still desperately unhappy. But there was a little light at the end of the tunnel and that was the fact that my three-month trial period at Finsbury was nearly up.

Things had been on a downward spiral at work. My paperwork was slipping and my overall performance was terrible compared with what I was achieving before. I was constantly in trouble over one thing or another, but I had simply stopped caring. Nothing was important for me any more. Everything seemed small and insignificant compared to my experiences in July.

I had been having a lot of trouble concentrating and remembering things in the short term. I would arrange to take a statement or have a suspect coming back on bail and then it would completely slip my mind. I tried keeping a diary – something that I had never had to do before – but I would even forget to look in it.

It was like being on autopilot. Every day was like the last and I couldn't have told you what I had done from one to the next. I would go into work, just to be there and be busy, but I would avoid being in the office at all costs. If there was no one about to work with, then I would go out on my own. This is dangerous for a copper working in north London, but I simply didn't care.

I put in my application to leave on the very morning that my trial period ended at Finsbury. I bit the bullet and cited my real reasons for wanting to leave. I assumed that the truth would at least make people aware that I was having more difficulties than I was letting on. I think now that it was my first subconscious cry for help.

The email that I got back surprised and shocked me. In my application, I had mentioned that I was having difficulties and that I was worried about my current state of mind. The reply expressed concern about the fact I was working at all – it sounded like the sender was trying to cover their own arse, just in case I lost it on the street. This infuriated me, and to top it off I still didn't have any word about whether I was to be moved, only a suggestion that my request would be passed up the chain of command to be considered.

The next couple of weeks I was in a thunderous mood. I was hearing nothing about my request and assumed that it had just been given a cursory glance and filed under

'Bin!' I feel sorry now for the guys I was working with at the time; some days I didn't even talk to them. I would come into work, grab my gear, and go out on my own in the first car available. I only felt at ease when I was on my own and working. I simply didn't want to be with others because I felt they did not understand me and never asked the right questions.

My work out on the ground had not slipped at all, unlike my paperwork. I could still deal with any incident that I was faced with, and this was the only time that I felt like my old self. As a police officer, when you are dealing with an incident it becomes the centre of your world at that moment. It usually takes a lot of thinking and you need the ability to make quick, positive and impartial decisions. This blocks everything else out. You think about nothing else and that was exactly what I wanted. I was not emotionally involved.

It was a couple of weeks before I got my first reply to my transfer request. I was to meet with a senior officer and a member of civilian staff from the Human Resources department at our area headquarters. I knew the officer that I was to be meeting and was not looking forward to it. I had had dealings with him before and knew him not to be very open to the opinions of the lower ranks. But it was a step in the right direction and I had a week to work out what I was going to say to the man.

The day finally arrived and I had made a big effort to look my best. I did not want this man's pity, I just wanted him to see things from my point of view and to realise that this move was the best thing for my welfare so that I could continue on my road to recovery and get back to being my normal self. I needed to convey the fact that I was desperately unhappy in my present post and did not know how much longer I could function in that role.

The meeting started with the formal introductions and the outlining of what was to be discussed. It was quite a dry affair and I could hear that what this officer was saying to me came straight out of the handbook. The Human Resources guy was there to record the minutes of the meeting and mediate between the two of us.

I started by explaining the reasons that I wanted to leave and expressed my displeasure in being moved in the first place after my traumatic experience. I stated that my orders to move should have been reassessed after the bombings had taken place and at least delayed until it was ascertained what effect this event had taken on me. I thought this a very reasonable point at the time and have since had this opinion supported by several Occupational Health experts, but for some reason I think that it was taken as a direct challenge on the decisions that the force had made.

I felt the officer was getting defensive with me, when I was simply expressing my opinion in what I thought was a very reasonable manner. At one stage, after I had raised another point, he told me that he disagreed with me and then added that he was trying very hard to keep the meeting welfare-orientated and not turn it into a 'discipline issue'. I was stunned. This man was not listening – or at least, it appeared to me, not hearing anything that I was trying to say.

What I heard next really took me aback. I was told that those in the room and the senior management had the impression that I had used the transfer to Finsbury Park as an excuse to go on the response-driving course in north Wales. My interviewer went on to suggest that now I had the qualification it looked as if I was trying to get out of Finsbury as fast as possible.

I was furious, but would not show it. I felt like this man was really laying into me, I was being backed into a corner, everything that I mentioned seemed to me as if he was turning into an attack on my professionalism; I was worried that my concerns were not going to be taken into account.

I tried to defend myself on numerous occasions, and was determined not to feel intimidated. I had been in a disciplined service all my life; I knew exactly when I was fighting a losing battle and when to keep my mouth shut. I simply sat there, trying to look as impassive as possible and not show any kind of reaction. I made rebuttals when I could and kept my cool.

All the time, it felt like he was trying to get a reaction out of me, but there was no way that I was going to let that happen. I kept my cool even though I was seething inside. Looking back, it seems that when he saw that I had said all I was going to and that he was going to get no reaction from me at all, I was curtly dismissed so that the two men could confer about what issues had been brought to light in the interview.

I stood up casually and walked out, smiling at them pleasantly as I did. As soon as the door was shut, however, I stormed out of the building and had a smoke in the most private place that I could find. I was livid. I was proud I had kept my cool, though: I hadn't given him anything to act on and I had to take that away from this experience at least.

I finished my cigarette quickly and rushed back to wait outside the door. I wasn't going to keep him waiting for me, I was going to be standing right there, smiling, when he opened the door. I was summoned back in and was expecting the worst. I had been dragged over the coals and thought that there was no way that I was going to have my request considered, let alone granted. I had resigned myself to that fact already and all I was interested in now was keeping my dignity and walking out of there with my chin up.

I sat back down in my seat and had to endure what felt like a longer-than-necessary silence while papers were needlessly shuffled and glanced at. Then I was told that my request was to be granted.

At that moment in time I felt like I was floating. If I had to describe my emotions at that time in one word it would be 'elated'. I was going back to my friends; I was going back to where I felt comfortable. I was not going to feel so isolated any more.

They told me that it would take three weeks to process the transfer, but that was a drop in the ocean for me. I was going back and that is what counted. I thanked the two men for their time and left the room with a spring in my step.

I skipped out of the building and went back to work; I was eager to leave Finsbury on a positive note. I had had a reputation as a good officer before I had arrived there, but my circumstances had contributed towards my tainting that a little; now I had a chance to do something about that before I left. I felt good. I didn't realise at the time that I was just avoiding my issues by moving again and I realise now that I could have been perfectly happy at Finsbury if I had addressed my problems as I have now. I was using it as an excuse for feeling the way I did. Admittedly, some of the circumstances of the move had not helped me, but I cannot blame them completely for the decline in my mental health. What was actually happening was that I was getting over the initial shock of the event and post-traumatic stress disorder was creeping in.

Chapter Twenty-Seven

LIAISONS

Despite my good intentions, I felt like I was treading water again at Finsbury Park. I was working well, but I was only thinking about the move back to the West End. At the time, it felt like it was the solution to all of my problems and that I would be miraculously fixed when I got back there. It seems irrational now, but back then I was clutching at straws. I was to have other things to take my mind of this for the time being, though.

Gill and I had been talking on the phone – not often, but I was getting used to her being a part of my life. It was easier only talking on the phone because I didn't have to look into her eyes and be reminded of things so vividly. She was expressing a really keen interest in meeting the rest of the team that I had worked with that day and having a drink with us all.

I stalled her and put this off for a while, I was still trying to define what kind of relationship I was going to have with this woman. I had spoken to some of the other guys about her and they were of the same opinion as me about the whole thing – i.e. that it might not be entirely healthy to see her outside a professional capacity. We didn't know what she was like at this stage and were unsure what the boundaries of our relationship would be. As police officers we are wary of everything and discretion is always the first instinct.

It was November 2005 by this time and I had been invited to attend St Paul's Cathedral for a memorial service to commemorate those who had lost their lives back in July. I'd got togged up in my dress uniform and had the rare opportunity to put on my medals. I remember being very excited about this; the Queen and the Prime Minister were going to be there along with other important dignitaries. A few noses had been put out of joint about the lack of invitations that had been made available to the force and in some respect the force's choice as to who received them. Of all the people I'd worked with on the day, only a few of us were going.

We were driven down to St Paul's in some of our vehicles and when we arrived I was amazed to see how many people were there. There were representatives from all of the emergency services, relatives of the deceased and some of the victims from the day. The cathedral was full to bursting.

I had seen Gill and Joe on my way in – they were sitting outside a coffee shop just outside the cathedral gates. I really wanted to say hello, but the day was already stirring a lot of emotion for me and I didn't think I could handle meeting her only for the second time then and there. Even though we had spoken on the phone, the memory of the reaction that I had experienced in Richmond was very fresh in my mind.

This was the first time that I had been in St Paul's. It is breathtaking; the high painted ceiling and the stone carvings are spectacular. I couldn't have thought of a more fitting venue for this service. The security, however, was immense. I have worked in the uniformed services all my adult life and could spot the plain-clothes officers and security operatives everywhere. No one's ID was left unchecked; even those in full uniform were checked thoroughly before being let in and seated.

The service was a very emotional one. It started once Her Majesty and the Prime Minister arrived and the national anthem had been sung. All the way through, I had been fighting off the tears. It brought a lot of what I felt inside to the surface – in particular, visions of the poor souls that we had had to leave on that train. Looking around me, I could see the families of those people and it broke my heart to watch them grieve. Afterwards, I went straight to the pub.

I heard from Gill in the next few days after the service. She told me that she had met so many people that had been involved in her rescue, but she had not met anyone that had carried her off the train apart from me and she was desperate to do so. I couldn't put it off any longer. Besides, it was only a few weeks to the wedding and I had to make my final decision as to whether I was going or not. This involved seeing her again.

The team that I had been working with in July all meet in a pub close to our home station for a serious drink every fifth Tuesday, the day that fits in best with our shift pattern. I suggested to Gill that this would be the best time for her to meet all of us out of work. She was thrilled and promised to be there and buy us a drink. OK, this was great – now all I needed to do was tell the team what I had arranged...

I approached the guys about it the next time I managed to get down to their station. My plans met with a mixed reaction. While everybody wanted to meet Gill, they were all concerned about the arrangement. It is very rare for police officers to meet people that they help outside their working environment and people feel uncomfortable about it for a range of different reasons.

In all the time that I have been a police officer, I have never heard of this happening before. It is common for officers to be heavily involved in helping and rescuing people from a variety of situations but the most contact that I had heard of, or seen first hand, was a letter sent to a police station thanking an officer or a group of officers for their actions and their help. Ours is a very thankless job sometimes.

The night of the meeting came and I was a bag of nerves. The whole team were in the pub and had been since three that afternoon. Gill could only make it around six o'clock, so we were waiting for her to arrive. Normally three hours in the pub for us would inevitably mean that we would all be steaming drunk, but we were all on our best behaviour for this occasion and had kept it very low key in anticipation of her arrival.

My phone rang later in the evening. It was Gill. She was just around the corner in a taxi and would be arriving shortly. I can't really describe how nervous I was. I really wanted everyone on the team to meet and like this woman, because she was a symbol of all we had achieved on that day; even the officers that had not been at Russell Square had all played their parts at other scenes. Also, I knew how important it was to Gill and I wanted her to feel welcome within the group. I hoped that we could have a normal evening of drinking and chatting.

Normality was very important to me back then. So much had changed within me and so much had happened that was out of the ordinary that I just wanted everything to go back to the way it was. At the time, I was of the opinion that I wanted everyone to carry on as though that day had never happened. I thought that the best thing my efforts could have achieved was for everyone to continue as they were before. I had even said to Gill during one of our conversations on the phone that the one thing that I hoped for was that she would go back to work and carry on like she had planned to do before that bomb took her legs. However, I didn't know the woman back then and I didn't know that I had changed as a person so much. I could never have known that our lives would become so intertwined, so different from anything I could ever have imagined.

Her taxi arrived and again I was staggered to see her step out onto the pavement. This really was a remarkable woman.

It was a big enough achievement to be standing two months after the event; now only another month had passed but she was walking towards me, albeit with the help of a stick.

Also with her that day were Gill's brother Graham and her sister-in-law Jo. They had been in the country from Australia for a while now. I was to find out during the course of the evening that they had flown over to be by Gill's side when she was in hospital and had returned for the memorial service. I got to know them that evening and I can tell you that they are both wonderful people. Graham is a very serious character but was so generous with his thanks to us that evening that you could almost feel what he was trying to say even though he was struggling for the words. Jo, on the other hand, is the complete opposite. Very rarely in my life have I ever met someone so open and full of energy. She was a hit with the guys and was to leave the pub that night at least three sheets to the wind.

Gill and I walked into the pub together; I was holding her elbow, though she clearly didn't need my help. All the team stood as she entered and no one said anything for a moment. My nerves were already frayed and I was convinced that I had made the wrong decision by organising the get-together. I took the initiative, though, and started making the introductions – and then everything fell into place. Gill started hugging everyone, being warm and friendly and the evening took off from there.

The drink and the conversation flowed; everyone was laughing. Mainly we spoke about *that* day, but Gill and her family were interested in our families and our backgrounds and never once did anyone get upset or sombre about our individual experiences; we just had a good time.

I think that Gary and Jo found a common interest that night, because they both sat rooted to the spot drinking all evening. They became louder and louder and the conversation became more colourful as the drinks disappeared.

I spent a lot of the time that night standing to one side letting everyone get on with it and watching the gathering that I had arranged. I had met Gill already, we had spoken on the phone; this was everyone else's chance to get to know this extraordinary woman. But every now and again she would catch my eye and smile or take my hand and squeeze it and I could tell that she was so grateful to have this opportunity to say thank you to everyone who had played a part in that day. The strange thing was that she had made the night seem so natural. There was a little bit of awkwardness in the beginning, but she had overcome that by being so open and normal about the whole thing.

The whole evening went better than I ever could have hoped. By the time Gill and her family were ready to leave, everyone was drunk and having a good time. Even those of us who do not normally come to the pub were still there and enjoying themselves. It was a huge success and that made me very happy. Perhaps, after all, I could have Gill as part of my life; perhaps it would not be as strange as I had initially thought.

When it started to get late, Gill said her goodbyes and I walked her out to the waiting taxi. She told me that she had also invited Big Ray to the wedding as well and I was pleased. At least now, if I were to go, then I wouldn't have to do it on my own. The fact that the night had gone so well and was not too weird had already convinced me that I was going to go. I had to see this thing through to the end and seeing the woman that I had saved walk down the aisle seemed like a fitting conclusion to the ordeal. It might even give me some kind of closure – and I was desperately seeking that.

Gill hugged me and it felt like she didn't want to let me go. We stood out in that cold street in the West End holding each other, oblivious to what was around us. It wasn't a lovers' embrace or one you would share with a family member or friend; it was pure relief. For me, it was the fact that she was alive and the simple fact that I was able to do it at all: that I could physically hold her in my arms, that all I had been through that day had a positive outcome and that all the torment in my mind was for something. She had her life and that was all the thanks that I needed to make it through my pain. To this day, I still see Gill as my crowning achievement. To be able to play a part in giving someone their life back is the most worthwhile thing that I have ever taken part in and I am sure that I will feel that way for the rest of my days.

After Gill had left, I went back into the pub. Of course, she was the main topic of conversation and everyone was of the opinion that she was a genuine and lovely person. She had become a kind of team mascot for us, a symbol of all our hard work and personal sacrifice.

We stayed in the pub until it closed – and got absolutely

smashed! Not one of us walked out in a straight line and everyone had sore heads come the morning. I couldn't have asked for a better outcome and even felt a little silly for having worried so much about the whole thing.

Chapter Twenty-Eight

THE WEDDING

It was now the run-up to Christmas and things were getting busy at work. I had finally got my transfer back to the West End and was excited to be back. I wasn't working with the same team, but it was nice to be in familiar surroundings again. The guys that I was working with seemed decent enough. It was a young, inexperienced team, but that suited me as I had ambition again and wanted promotion. It would be easier for me to do it in an environment that I could shine in.

All in all, things were looking up. I was in the place that I wanted to be in, I still saw my old team nearly every day and I was in a position where I could go far in my work. I had everything that I had wanted before; everything that I thought would pull me out of the rut that I was in and help me get better. So why was I still so messed up in the head?

It seemed that with every day that passed my fuse was getting shorter and shorter. I had gone from being quite an easy-going bloke to a bit of a grumpy old sod. I would get incredibly frustrated with the young officers that I worked with because they would make a small mistake or simply not do something the way that I would have. Most of it was down to inexperience – we have all been there at one time or another, it was nothing to get angry about – but I couldn't help myself.

At first, I thought that I was just uptight because it was coming up to Gill and Joe's wedding. The impending day was weighing heavily on my thoughts and I was getting really nervous. I knew that her family would be there and that everyone would be talking about the bombings – in fact, that would be the theme for the whole day – and I didn't think that I was strong enough for that yet. It all seemed just a little too much: I didn't want to put myself in a position where I could show any emotion. I felt like I was holding back the tide and, if a little bit leaked out, then I was afraid that it would all just gush out and I would make a spectacle of myself.

The actual wedding day was 10 December. In the weeks preceding the day, I must have changed my mind fifty times as to whether I would be going or not, but the fact that Ray was going as well finally clinched it for me. I used him as an excuse because I couldn't let him go on his own.

The wedding itself was in a small church in the City of London. You wouldn't know it was there unless you were shown; it is kind of mixed in with a group of really old cottages in a private road that is separated from the rest of London by a large set of cast-iron gates.

As Ray and I approached the entrance to the road, I was taken aback by the amount of press who were gathered by the gate. Ray and I had our photos taken repeatedly as we showed our invitations to the security guard. I didn't even look at them. I just strode up the road towards the church and did my best to look as moody and unphotogenic as possible. I was so surly that when the wedding photographer asked me for a photo on the way into the church I told her to fuck off because I thought she was paparazzi. Oops!

The inside of the church was packed; by the time I arrived it was standing-room only. People were jammed into every available space. I always get nervous in churches – I have only been in them a handful of times and I always feel like I am under examination when I do. It is probably just my overactive imagination, but the places give me the creeps. But even for someone who does not particularly like churches, I had to admire this one. The place was very old, decorated with beautiful stone carvings and had flags and banners over the walls. It actually felt quite inviting and warm, whereas normally I hate the cold, empty feel of a church. The choir were singing from a balcony directly over my head and you would have had to be a very hard soul indeed not to be caught up in the atmosphere.

It wasn't a long wait before the service started. The organist started and everyone stood. I could just see the top of Joe's head at the front of the church, but was craning my head around the mass of people between me and the aisle so

197

I could catch a glimpse of Gill as she walked in. There she was – and she looked beautiful! She was walking down the aisle holding the arm of her brother Graham.

Gill looked stunning in her long, flowing ivory dress and I couldn't take my eyes off her. I couldn't get over the contrast between that first time I had seen her and now – if I didn't know better, I would have said those were two different people.

The service lasted for what seemed an absolute age. I had never been to a Catholic wedding before this one and I didn't realise that it would all be in Latin and last about a week! I am sure that what the bloke in the robe was saying was very interesting, but not being able to fathom any of what he was saying kind of made my mind wander.

I had noticed, both in the church and outside, that a lot of people were looking and pointing at me. Obviously, all of these people knew Gill and they had probably seen me on the documentary with her. I was getting curious looks from all over the place and random people I didn't know were continually smiling at me. It made me feel very uncomfortable indeed. I spent most of the service staring around the church and trying to avoid all those pairs of eyes; I felt like I was on display, and was not liking it a bit. I would look to the front when I heard someone say something in English, though there wasn't really much of that.

During the proceedings, we found out that the press were not the only ones who had gotten wind of Gill and Joe's wedding. They had received letters of congratulations from the Archbishop of Westminster and the Pope, of all people. This really was a high-profile affair.

When the ceremony finished, we all filed outside and prepared to go to the reception. Gill and Joe found Ray and me and started to introduce us to their family and friends. I was overwhelmed by the emotion these people showed towards us, and didn't know what to say to them. They were thanking us for saving Gill's life and doing it with such feeling that I was completely taken back.

I really didn't know how to respond to them. As far as I was concerned, I hadn't done anything that magnificent that day – I had just been doing my job and that's all there was to it. At the time it almost felt that they were thanking me for something as mundane as giving a speeding ticket. I never thought that I had gone above and beyond, I was just faced with a task to perform and I had done it. It is only now, over a year after the event, that what we did on 7 July 2005 has sunk in. It is only when I consider the people whose lives we gave back that I gain any perspective on what was achieved that day. People will live and grow old because of the work of the emergency services; they will have children and grandchildren because they were given another chance by people who were just doing their job. If you ask me, it is a very special occupation to have when you can have a positive impact on people's lives like this, no matter how infrequently the opportunities come along.

After a few minutes of photographs and handshakes, it was time to go to the reception. Joe is a bit of a bus fanatic and he had organised two Routemasters to take the wedding party to the Wapping Power Station, where the reception was being held. One of these buses was the traditional red, but the other was the bright colour of gold. It really was special and everyone seemed to love the idea.

We all boarded and the buses set off, but as we exited the gates out onto the main road, we were swamped with press. Some of them were like animals hanging off every part of the vehicles that they could. There were flashbulbs going off in every window and one really persistent one even jumped onto the platform at the back of the bus and started to take pictures inside. What an invasion of privacy. Gill and Joe were not celebrities, they were normal people who had been through a living hell in the previous six months and were now trying to get married in peace.

Once we had cleared the mob of photographers, we made our way out of the city and to the reception. When we arrived, I must admit that I wasn't very impressed. The outside looked like an abandoned industrial building and really quite depressing. I could only guess what the inside looked like.

Ray and I were still sticking close to each other and dealing with the people that were coming up to us together. Now that we were out of the church and in a more informal atmosphere, more people were coming up to us and thanking us. They obviously made a beeline for me because they had seen me on the TV, but I was very quick to tell them about Ray's involvement so that perhaps they would talk to him and not me. I wasn't being rude, but I really didn't know what to say to these people; it was all getting a bit much and I was starting to get stressed.

Eventually, Ray and I joined the queue to get in. I am not

sure what I expected the place to look like when I got in there, but nothing could have prepared me for what I was going to see; the contrast to the outside was staggering. The walls of the reception room were bare brick; it all looked very old and very worn. The room was quite dark, lit by dozens of candles; in the centre of the room was a huge real Christmas tree and completely covering the floor were tons of salt granules, to imitate snow. To top all of this off, there was a choir singing in the corner and the waitresses were walking round giving out mulled wine. It was like a winter wonderland and I was reminded of *The Lion the Witch and the Wardrobe* from when I was a kid. I think that it was the most atmospheric room I have ever been in – before or since. The whole thing just felt warm and happy; you could feel the good mood of everyone in the room and I was soaking it up.

I think that I drank about three large glasses of wine in the first thirty minutes I was there. I was incredibly nervous and was really stressed about all the people coming and talking to me. Needless to say, it didn't take me long to start feeling a little fuzzy.

Gill and Joe kept coming over to us and we had our picture taken with them a few times, but for the most part we were stuck in that room surrounded by people who knew who we were but who we didn't have a clue about. I even had one person crying as they were talking to me.

This must sound awful! I am not, for a moment, discrediting the way that those people were feeling and what they were trying to say, but I'm trying to explain how someone as shy as me felt so awkward in that situation.

Everyone wanted to say thank you to us for saving the life of their loved one, but how do you take that thanks? It is not like you are being thanked because you lent a mate some money or you went to the shop for your mum to get some milk. You are being thanked for saving a life – how do you respond? Badly, in my case: I just got drunk!

The thing is, the more I drank the worse I was starting to feel. The room that had been so comfortable before was starting to feel cramped and hot; the dark was starting to remind me not of a cosy Christmas atmosphere but of a Tube tunnel lit only with emergency lighting. At one point, I was talking to Gill and when she looked me in the eyes her face changed: she went from being the beautiful woman that had walked down the aisle in the church to being pale through lack of blood, with her damp hair plastered to her face with sweat. I had to close my eyes and force the image away, and try to get a grip of myself. It was exactly this that I was afraid of happening; I simply had no control over these images.

The party moved upstairs to the restaurant after a while as it was time to eat. I was quite wasted by this point and starting to think I was the funniest bloke on the planet, which happens when I'm loaded and more so when I'm nervous and having difficulty dealing with a situation. Luckily, Ray had not lost his rag with me yet for making jokes at his expense, so I sat with him and a load of other coppers we had met downstairs.

For some reason, I was starting to get really anxious now. I think that it may have been the drink, but I wasn't doing too well. All I had been doing from the time that the wedding had started was talk about the bombings, it was all people wanted to know about and it was really was starting to get to me. I don't really know what else I expected, but I could feel myself getting more and more upset the more I talked about it, and the more upset I got the more I drank. I was on that slippery slope again, petrified that I was going to lose it. I avoided talking to anyone, sat at the table and ate staring at my plate. Ray seemed happy enough, so I left him to it and went outside for a cigarette, but even outside I couldn't escape it. I was bumping into people out there who would introduce themselves by saying, 'Hi, you looked busy inside so I didn't come over but I'm so and so and I just want to say thank you for all you have done…' I had to get out of there! I had to escape before I did or said something stupid.

I didn't even say goodbye. I just left. I felt so claustrophobic that I simply ran out. I did look for Gill before I left, but she seemed so happy that I didn't want to do anything to put a downer on her day; besides, I wouldn't be missed. I went out into the car park, jumped the ten-foot gate that had been locked to keep the press out and walked to the nearest DLR station. As soon as I left that building it was like having a weight lifted off my chest. Inside, I had been in a bad way; I had started to get the same king of feeling that I'd had when I walked into a Tube station. It was the panicky flashback thing that was making my life a misery. All the day did for me was serve as one big reminder of the day I was trying to forget and now I was really messed up because I had put myself through it. I should have gone with my first instinct and stayed away. Now most of Gill and Joe's family probably thought I was a right weirdo.

I was pretty pissed as I was making my way back into central London, but I was of the opinion that, given the circumstances, I was not pissed enough. I needed to forget what I had just been through and get thoroughly wasted. I could feel a session coming on and I knew exactly where to find it.

As luck would have it, my friend Chrissie was having a birthday party. Chrissie is the girl that runs the pub that we all drink in after work. She and I get on like a house on fire, so I knew that if I went out with her I would have a whale of a time and be able to forget all my woes for the one night at least.

We hit it pretty hard that night. Most of it is just a blur because I drank myself into a stupor. The first clear memory that I have is of leaving a nightclub behind King's Cross at nine o'clock in the morning with Chrissie and a few friends from work. If there is one thing that I can say I do well it is letting off steam, and it was definitely needed on this occasion.

All in all, I am glad that I went to the wedding now. It was not a very nice day for me because it brought back so many horrible memories, but at least I was there to see my friends tie the knot. I just wish that I had been in a better state of mind so that I could have enjoyed it more.

I feel bad now that I missed most of the reception and that I left in such a hurry. I found out afterwards that I was missed, after all. I was mentioned during the speeches, but when everyone turned around to look for me I was gone. It was probably for the best, though: I think that would have finished me off. I missed out on quite a lot and Gill was upset that I left. I know that she understands, as she knows what kind of person I am now and she knows that I do not like the attention – the kind that I was getting that day, anyway. She is a very understanding woman and one thing she has maintained from the start is that she accepts me for who I am and what I do and she wouldn't change that for the world. I think that is a very rare thing to find and I am lucky to have her as my friend.

Chapter Twenty-Nine .

FALLING DOWN

Christmas came and went; I worked the whole thing, because I really couldn't see the point of being at home, as I was living on my own. I was more interested working the bank holidays and earning some extra money. I had not really talked to Gill and Joe much because they were on their honeymoon in Australia, although they did phone me on Christmas Day to say they were having a barbecue.

Christmas was especially difficult for me that year. It was the second one that I had spent on my own since the separation from my wife and would have been bad enough on its own without all the emotional baggage that I was carrying from the bombings. It was at times like this that I missed my son the most, and I am afraid to say my wife as well. My family was my life, all I lived for.

I have always loved Christmas, but this year was a bit of a

bah-humbug period for me. I couldn't find anything to get excited about. My mum and I had had a run-in a few months before and were not talking, so I wasn't going to be spending it with her. My sister has her own family and I didn't wanted to lumber myself on them during the season of good will. I was not the happiest person to be around and just wanted to stay out of everybody's way. I ended up working all through the period and earning as much money as I could. I popped in and saw my sister and her family for a few hours but that was it.

I started a set of shifts on Christmas Eve and did not have a day off until 2 January. They were mostly 12-hour shifts and the whole season passed me by. I do not know what else I could have done. If I had stopped to think for more than a few minutes over that period, I think that I would have fallen apart. I have never felt so alone in my entire life. But I got through it the same way that I did everything else: I ignored it until it went away.

In the months that followed, things kind of levelled out for me. I still had the same problems, but I had now been coping with them for so long that had managed to adapt and fit them into my life and operate at a level that was nearly normal. If you were looking from the outside in, all you would have picked up was that I had become a little grumpier of late. But seeing as I never let people get to know me that well, and the people that could get close to me at this stage were nonexistent, no one really noticed. I was still turning up for work and on time, I was still working all the shifts that I could get my hands on, I was fitting quite well into my new team and had found a place for myself there. I had even been promoted to acting sergeant and was running my team at work. Everything seemed normal, but inside I was a wreck.

By now, I had got to the point where I just wanted to run away. It was getting harder and harder to keep things bottled up and as a result my temper was flaring more regularly.

I had been looking into doing volunteer work abroad and taking a career break to go travelling because I didn't think I could handle it in this country any more. Even coming to work was a chore now. I was finding it increasingly difficult to get out of bed and falling asleep was torturous every day. I needed to get out, I had begun to wonder at the start of every shift if this was going to be the day when I completely lost it and landed myself in the shit. Coming to London was a constant reminder: everything seemed to bring back memoria of something about 7 July, and I wasn't sure how much longer I could handle it.

Through all my pain and my anguish, when I was struggling just to function on a day-to-day basis, there was one thing that broke my heart more than anything else. It was not the nightmares the flash backs or my feelings of guilt. It was the separation from my son and feeling utterly alone because of it.

At the time of the bombings, I had been separated from my wife for ten months. She left me because our relationship was beyond repair, but when she left she took my son with her and he was my reason for living. I cannot put into words how much I miss him; it is like a hole in my heart that refuses to heal.

I had been on my own for ten months before that morning in July and I was still very raw and struggling to cope with the loss of my family. They were all I had known for the entirety of my adult life and during the early stages of my recovery that loss weighed heavily on me and caused me a great deal of pain.

My son was born in October 2000 just eighteen months after our wedding. My wife and I were only nineteen but wanted a family as we thought it would complete our lives at the time.

I always said that if I had children then I would only do it when I felt secure enough. I did not want to raise a child in a broken home and have that child experience the things I did growing up. I know now that I couldn't have foreseen the future but that we were probably too young to be thinking about such things.

The night that Brook was born was one of the happiest of my life. I will never forget first seeing his wrinkled little body; I broke down in tears immediately and didn't regain the power of speech for about a quarter of an hour. I cut his cord and held him in my arms and for the first time in my life I felt the purity of a father's love for his son. I knew from that moment on that this boy was the love of my life and that nothing could ever change that.

I didn't get to spend long with Brook when he was newborn. Only a few days later I flew out to Bosnia on an operational tour and did not see my son for many months. By the time I returned he was almost a toddler and I couldn't help but feel that I had missed out on so much.

After that separation, I completely doted on my son. He became the centre of my world and there were no lengths that I would have not gone to for his happiness. I didn't spoil him but I always played with him and showed him as much attention as I could – my wife and I both did.

As a result of this constant stimulation, he developed very quickly and turned into a very bright and sprightly young boy who was a pleasure to be around. I used to do as much as I could with him and even took him fishing a couple of times at that very early age. I wanted to expose him to all the things that I loved in the hope that when he was older he would love them too and we could do them together.

For the four years I spent like this, I couldn't have been happier. Things with my wife and me were far from perfect but my relationship with Brook more than made up for what was lacking in my marriage and I was content. He became my reason for living and everything that I did in life was for him.

However, I may have been content to live like this but my wife was not. I think that probably makes her a stronger person than me for doing something about it, but I am still unhappy about the way that she went about it. It came completely out of the blue for me. One minute, everything is going really well. I have made a good start to my new job as a police officer and I am enjoying it, I have a loving son whom I adore and I am happy with life. The next minute, I have nothing apart from an empty house and a broken heart.

I want to be angry with her for leaving me, but I cannot.

I want to hold a grudge, but I do not see the point. What is done is done and my life is probably better for it. My wife and I did not make each other happy and Brook was the only thing that was holding us together. To have feelings of negativity towards her would only be a waste of energy and it would accomplish nothing. I honestly hope that she is happy and has found in her life what was lacking when she and I were married.

It is always the little things that you miss the most. Brook used to wake me up every morning by jumping on the bed and gave me a big hug whenever I walked in the door. He was always asking me to play with him and was always interested in what I was doing. Whenever I went out, he wanted to come and he really looked up to me as I was his dad, the ex-soldier and policeman, I used to hear him telling his friends about me and I used to nearly burst with pride. He was a real daddy's boy. When these things were gone, I felt utterly alone. I never took him for granted, he was the light of my life and without him I was in a very dark place.

It is difficult to explain how this affected me when I was suffering after the bombings. It definitely enhanced the feeling of isolation that I had, but above all I felt that my life was completely devoid of love. When I was at my lowest, it was made worse by the fact that Brook was not there; it was just something else to be upset about when I thought that I couldn't get any more miserable.

Brook is a very loving child and I know that if he had seen me upset he would have given me a cuddle or asked me what was wrong because that is the kind of son he is. He could never have understood my pain, but he would have detected something because he is a special child.

I cannot help but think that if he had been around me I wouldn't have suffered as much as I did. In Brook, I find a reason to live and I think that if he was around at the time I would have found a reason to cope. I think that I would have held it together because of him.

Still, to this day, nothing fills the hole in my life that Brook has left but for the first time since my family left I feel strong enough to do something about it. There have been days in the period since the bombings when I haven't even had the mental strength to get out of bed, let alone fight for access to my son, and that weighs heavily on me. But now things have changed and I am driven.

I love my son more than words can describe and all I want from life is to have a relationship with him again. I want to watch him grow into the fine young man that I know he will be. I want to love him, guide him and give him the benefit of my experiences, so perhaps he will not make the same mistakes that I have. But above all, I want to be his dad again.

I managed to plod through to April on a kind of autopilot; I can't really remember much that happened during this period now. Each day seemed to fade seamlessly into the next and each one was a struggle to get through. I knew that I couldn't keep it up forever, but I was at a complete loss as to what I could actually do. I was waiting for something to send me over the edge; I didn't have to wait long.

It happened when I was working a late shift around mid-

April. I normally love late shifts, because they are busy and the time flies. I was working with a friend of mine called Zona; she had transferred from Hampshire constabulary and was on the team that I joined on my return from Finsbury. She and I hit it off straight away; she was a great laugh and spoke her mind at every turn. And there is the fact that she is a really good cop and I respected her for that and enjoyed working with her as a result. We always had a good giggle working together and never ran out of things to talk about when we were patrolling London in the car. She was my favourite person to work with and I am glad that she was in the car on this particular evening, because she helped take my mind off things at the time.

It was quite late in the shift when the call came out – I think around nine o'clock. Zona and I were stuck in traffic on Oxford Street and were a little bored, as we had not been that busy all night. Normally, when a call comes out near the end of your shift, you are reluctant to take it – it means that you are going to get tied up with something and not be able to get home because you will miss your last train – but this one was a little different.

The message went out over the radio that a person had been struck by a train in north London on the mainline tracks quite close to Tottenham. This is not unusual by any stretch of the imagination. It happens in London at least twice a week – mainly it is a suicide, sometimes it is an accident and occasionally someone is pushed. These incidents are part and parcel of our job and in the course of my career I have been to over twenty of them.

At first, Zona and I did not intend to go – this was way off our area, and other units would deal with it as it was their place to. But as time went on, it became evident that the control room could not raise enough units to go. The north London officers had been dealing with another incident and lots were still tied up with that. I looked at Zona and that is all it took: we were going. Zona told the control room over the radio and I turned on the blues and twos. I started weaving my way in and out of the traffic heading in the general direction while Zona found the location on the map. I had worked in Finsbury for only a short time, so I did not know this part of London that well. The incident had happened on a level crossing, so we had the nearest road name to go by.

As we were getting closer, the news over the radio got worse. A unit had turned up and discovered that, in fact, two people had been hit, and they were both teenagers. When the officer was asked if the victims were alive or not, the exact reply was, 'The bodies are far too disrupted for there to be any chance of life.' I knew by these few words that it was going to be a messy one and that it was going to be a very long night indeed.

I could feel the dread in the pit of my stomach as we neared the scene. Not only did I not want to see what was waiting for us at the end of our journey, this was the first time Zona had attended an incident of this nature and I didn't know how she was going to react. I had to keep it together for her sake as well as mine. She would be looking to me for guidance and support when we got there, I

215

couldn't show any kind of weakness in front of her. In fact, looking back, I am not entirely sure Zona needed anything from me that night; she handled herself very well.

We arrived about fifteen minutes after the call had gone out. I pulled the car into the access road that led to the crossing. It was in the middle of an industrial estate and I would never have found it without the map. I could see the other police vehicles parked at the end of the road and pulled up a short distance behind them. As I got out of the car, I thanked myself for putting my heavy jacket in before leaving the station; it was absolutely freezing cold and I remember thinking at the time how different the environment was to the tunnel at Russell Square.

Zona and I made our way to the tracks and liaised with the other officers on the scene. Immediately, I saw where one of the bodies was lying. It was off to one side of the tracks, about twenty yards from the crossing. Mercifully, somebody had covered it with a body bag. But I could see other smaller shadows in the dark around the corpse and knew they were smaller pieces of the body that had detached. As I looked farther up the track I could see the train. It had stopped roughly half a mile away and I could just make out the shape of it in the dark punctuated by the red lights on the rear.

I volunteered to do the track search with another officer from Finsbury whom I knew called Kat, leaving Zona with another officer to receive direction from the senior officer on the scene. Doing the track search is quite a grizzly job. It involves walking the track from the point of impact to the train looking for body parts so that they can be recorded and recovered at a later date. You maybe asking yourself why someone in my position would volunteer for a job like this, but the overriding factor for me at the time was that I desperately needed a fag!

Kat and I both smoked, so as soon as we were far enough up the track to be out of sight of anyone important, we sparked up. We walked the track for the half a mile and what we saw was carnage. The two teenagers had been struck by the train, which had been travelling on a fast part of the line. It was really hard to spot what we were looking for because of the dark and the narrow beam of my torch was not up to the job.

It is a very surreal experience doing a job like this. You will be walking along, chatting to your colleague, idly trying to act as normal as you can to disassociate yourself from what you are doing and then every couple of steps it would be, 'Oh look, there's something!' And then you would make a note of where it was and continue walking and chatting, battling with yourself to put the image of what you have just seen out of your head.

We walked the line until there was nothing left to find and I made a note in my pocket book of the nearest physical reference point so that when the body recovery took place the officers involved would know how far they had to go. After this was done, we decided to walk to the train to check on the welfare of the driver. He had already seen the police and given his first account of what had happened, but a friendly chat can often help take a driver's mind off things for a while in such a situation.

It is the drivers that really suffer the most at an incident like this. They have a front-row seat to someone else's death and sometimes when it happens they cannot face getting in the cab of a train again. I have heard of drivers on the Underground who have been involved in three or four 'one-unders' and it has left them with no option but to take a job in a station so they do not have to risk it happening to them again.

As Kat and I walked the length of the train, we could see all the passengers still inside. It was a late train and it was full of people returning home from nights out. All the time, I was shining my torch at the running gear underneath trying to spot any body parts that might have been caught up as the train passed over the victims. It struck me at this point how massive a train on the tracks is: you don't really notice it at train stations because of the platform, but when you are standing next to one at ground level, you get the full ideal of the scale of the thing. It is not surprising that they do so much damage when they hit a person.

At the front end of the train we stood and spoke to the driver. He was standing outside with a couple of workers from the railway and seemed OK, but I knew that once the shock wore off it would be a different story. He told us what had happened and for the first time I realised that this was not a suicide. It turned out in the end to have been a game of chicken gone wrong. What a waste of life: two young boys killed because they had a twisted idea that standing in front of a train for as long as they could would be fun.

We stood around talking for a while and I started to roll

another cigarette. It was quite dark where I was standing at the side of the train, so I thought I would use the lights at the front of the train to make things easier. But as I looked at one of the headlights I froze. So far, I had managed to keep everything together. I had seen all kind of gore in my walk up the tracks, but I had done a good job of disassociating myself from it. This was different.

The front of the train was a mess. I could see the point of impact now and for the first time in my police career I heaved and thought I was going to be sick. It was not pretty and what I saw completely cut down any defences that I had put up.

Once I let that one thing affect me, the rest of it started to flood in. In one instant I had become I wreck and just wanted out of there. I was no longer just doing my job; I was trying to keep my sanity. Every body part that I had just seen reminded me of the scene inside that Tube train, and as well as having to deal with the situation that I was in, I was having to deal with what I had seen during the bombings.

I'm sure I looked OK from the outside, because no one commented, but I made my excuses and headed back down the track as fast as I could, trying not to look at the floor, all the time chatting to Kat about anything other than the situation we were in. My heart rate and breathing had sped up in an instant and I could feel the adrenaline coursing through my body. I felt like I had on the day when I was carrying Gill. I am surprised that I lasted that long, but now all I wanted to do was get out of there. I was praying that there were more officers on the scene and we would be released to go back to our own area and be able to go home.

When I got back to the level crossing, I could see that the Scene of Crime officers had arrived. It is their job to photograph incident scenes and collect the body parts when they have been recorded. I approached one of them as he was unloading his kit from his van and told him what Kat and I had found on our track search. With this done, I set off to find Zona.

She was up the track a little and was guarding one of the bodies. Because it was such a big scene, an officer has to stand with the bodies so that they can be sure they are not moved or tampered with by anyone so that they can be recorded where they came to rest. Although the body was covered, it was surrounded by human debris from the force of the impact. It was a struggle not to look at these body parts and I found myself doing everything that I could to ignore their presence. I didn't have the adrenaline that I had during the bombings, I didn't have any tasks to perform, all I could do was stand there and have the images burnt into my memory.

We stood there for hours while the investigation was taking place. Every half an hour or so we would get a break so we could go and warm up in the car, but for the majority of the time we were stood trackside with this young man, and me trying not to imagine what was under the sheet, just feet from where I was standing.

I had turned into a chain smoker and was pacing up and down. I was so glad that I was with Zona, because she is one of the chattiest people I work with and without knowing it she was helping me out just by talking to me. I was doing my best to deal with the situation, but inside I was in pieces.

I knew that there had been a massive change in me since the bombings; the experience that I had been through on that day had completely stripped away the defences that I used to put up when dealing with a situation like this. Before, I had been able to attend incidents of this type and function easily – of course, they used to upset me, but nothing compared to what I was feeling on that night. Previously, I would have been able to do my job and not give the situation a second thought until after the event. I would go home and be upset for a day or two, but other things in my life would take over and the event would become nothing but a distant and nasty memory. Things had changed for me now; I could not disassociate myself from what I was doing. It seemed that every gruesome sight I witnessed would stab away at a part of me that felt very exposed and very raw.

As Zona and I were standing there, chatting and passing the time, I could see the Scene of Crime officer getting closer to where we were standing and I knew that the evening was winding down. He was marking every body part with a number and photographing them in order. The recovery starts after this is done, so I knew it wouldn't be long as we were standing near the end of the scene.

As he approached us, our relief started walking up the tracks towards us. It was our turn to go and sit in the car and get warm. Then it occurred to me: the photographer was going to want to lift the sheet on the body we were guarding and what was underneath was not something that I wanted to see. As it turned out, they all arrived at exactly the same time and I half ran from the scene as I saw them preparing to lift the sheet. I was about twenty yards away when I heard their reaction to what they saw. I was glad that I didn't stick around: that image will be branded into those officers' minds now, and I for one didn't need any more of those kind of images.

We were there for another couple of hours in total, swapping between standing in the cold and warming up in the car. We managed to get a cup of tea from a fast-food outlet just down the road, but it was all very routine. Once things started to wind down, the senior officer on the scene released us and thanked us for our help. I couldn't wait to get out of there; I had seen enough and was not looking forward to the prospect of going home on my own. I knew that I would be getting very little sleep that night.

By the time Zona and I returned to the police station, we had missed our last trains by a couple of hours. I had to borrow one of the unmarked cars from CID just to get us home. Zona lives in east London, so it is on my way home to drop her off just before I turn off to go through the Blackwall Tunnel. The drive back was a quiet one. Because I had been dealing with my own issues, I had completely forgotten that it was Zona's first time at an incident of this type. God knows what was going through her mind that night and I feel guilty now for not being as supportive as I should have been. But all I could think of during that time was wanting to be on my own so that I could concentrate on sorting my head out.

After dropping Zona off at her door, I headed for home. I

turned the stereo up and tried to lose my thoughts in the music, but it wasn't working. I didn't get far before I had to pull over. I had reached the dual carriageway, but I could feel my eyes filling with tears. I was on my own for the first time all night and I was breaking down.

I pulled over onto the hard shoulder, put my head on the steering wheel and sobbed. I had spent the entire duration of the incident battling with myself, trying to keep the awful images out of my head and trying my hardest to disassociate myself from what I was doing – and it had exhausted me. I couldn't believe how hard it had been to deal with the situation. As I have said before, I could handle this kind of stuff in the past, but now I felt helpless and weak.

I am not sure how long I was there for, but it was over half an hour. I cried so hard that my chest hurt and my eyes ached – but it was OK, because I was alone and no one could see me. I cried for the children who had lost their lives. I cried for the victims of the bombings. I cried for Gill, who had lost her legs. But most of all, I cried for myself. I cried because I was not the person that I used to be, I could not handle seeing these disturbing things any more and that ultimately meant I couldn't do my job properly. I didn't know where to turn. All I knew was that I couldn't put myself through this any more.

Chapter Thirty

WHY I DO
WHAT I DO

I think that at this point it is prudent to tell you why I do what I do and why I am still doing it. You would think that after all I had been through and the anguish I suffered afterwards that I would just give up on it and work in a nice air-conditioned office somewhere. But I still go to work every day because I don't think that I would be complete without it.

The thing is, I have always wanted to do something that mattered. I wanted to have a positive impact on the world we live in, no matter how small that impact may be. I know it sounds a bit cheesy but I have always thought this way. From my time in the army to now, I have always wanted to help shape the world we live in and do what I can to make it a better place in my own small way.

The events of 7 July 2005 have changed my life forever

and I am writing this now to tell the world about that day and the bravery and professionalism displayed by every member of the emergency services that took part in the rescue so far under the ground. It was an event that will stay with me for the rest of my days and despite the pain that it has caused me I am proud that I was there

Being a police officer gives you the opportunity to make a difference. You are out on the street every day trying to do the right thing, to help people and deal with the incidents that you are confronted with. I could not think of another job that is so varied and diverse. One minute you could be arresting a robber or a drunk; the next minute you could be giving CPR to an injured person or holding the hand of a young child who has lost their parents in the West End and is scared out of their wits.

These are just some of the examples of why I get up for work each morning. As corny as it sounds, they are the things that make me feel better about myself as a person and give me the motivation to carry on. A few people have questioned this of me in the last 18 months, but I know in my heart that I still love the feeling I get when I do something of worth.

People do not congratulate police officers for doing their job; as a matter of fact, even police officers rarely thank each other for doing a good job. But I do not need thanks for what I do. I have the sense of self-satisfaction, knowing that I have done things that have changed people's lives for the better – and maybe I have even saved a few.

This makes things worth it and I draw on it for strength

when I am at my lowest. For a while after the bombings, I and a few of the officers that I worked with were upset that we didn't get an MBE like some officers did or an official recognition for our efforts on that day. To be frank, we were actually quite bitter about it. But it didn't take me long to realise that that wasn't what I really wanted. I was just directing my anger anywhere I could and it was easy to focus on that one aspect of the situation. I had all the thanks that I needed when I saw Gill alive and standing when I met her, or when her husband and brother shook my hand. You can hold a medal in your hand, but all you can do is look at it – you can't feel it like you can someone's gratitude.

The way I see it, someone has to do the job we do. It is not the best job in the world, but it certainly isn't the worst. A lot of people dislike you for the job that you do and sometimes you are instantly judged when you tell people what you do for a living. But every now and again, the members of the emergency services get to do something great. They have the chance to save lives and turn chaos into order. The events of July 2005 may have torn me apart inside, but I wouldn't have given my place up in that tunnel to anyone else. What I and my friends achieved on that day can never be taken away from us for as long as we live.

Chapter Thirty-One

ENOUGH IS
ENOUGH

I went back to work after the incident in north London; I didn't know what else to do. I had locked myself in my flat for a couple of days and not seen a soul, but the time to reflect had not given me an answer to my problem. When I got back, though, I found I just couldn't function.

It seemed like my memory had been shot to bits: I could remember what I had done five years ago, but I couldn't remember what I had done five minutes ago. It was like I was walking around in a daze that I couldn't snap out of. Every day was a chore from start to finish and if I could get through one without making a mistake or forgetting to do something important, then I would count myself lucky.

I tried to hide it by being bolshy and pretending that I didn't care about the things I was getting wrong. But this just gave people the opinion that I didn't give a shit and not that

I couldn't function or cope. I was making things worse for myself and even being out and about in the car was not distracting me any more because I was having to concentrate so hard on getting things right.

I was getting more and more frustrated with myself. I have already mentioned that my temper had gotten bad before, but it was getting worse. I was taking it out on those around me and being very difficult to be with, let alone work with. Zona was the only one I could work alongside, the only one with whom I could keep my foul moods under control.

The moment when I lost it was not obvious to those around me. I had become a bit of an expert at hiding my feelings from the world. As far as anyone else was concerned, I was just a grumpy bastard – they didn't know what was going on underneath it all. But I can remember it as clear as day. It was a normal morning on shift and I was sitting in a briefing, getting ready for the start of the day. I felt rough anyway because I had been getting next to no sleep for as long as I can remember and had been drinking a bit more than usual to help me drop off. All that happened was the sergeant on duty that morning told me to put my tie on because I looked a mess. That was all, but it was the straw the broke my back. From the outside I probably looked a bit pissed off, though there was nothing unusual in that. But on the inside I was screaming at the top of my voice. It was all I could do to stop myself from shaking and in my mind's eye I had visions of me standing up and throwing the chair I was sitting on through the window.

How I managed to keep myself under control I don't

know. I just sat there seething for the remainder of the briefing, not saying a word and staring at the wall as if I could bring it down with a look. When the briefing was over, I walked out with everyone else. I got halfway down the corridor and turned back. I had to say something, there was no way that I could work today, there was no telling what I would do.

I walked into the sergeant's office and simply said to her: 'I've had enough, I can't work today, I'm going home.' With that I walked out with the promise that I would see the Occupational Health advisor when I could. I didn't give a shit about Occupational Health at the time, I just wanted to go home, but I phoned them anyway. At the time, I just considered it an arse-covering exercise so that I didn't get in trouble for going home. But the advisor asked me to come and see him in the office before I got on the train.

His office was in our area headquarters, which is on the Broadway near St James's Park. I waited outside to be seen and when I went in he asked me what the matter was so I told him straight. I was beyond caring by this point, so I told him everything about the bad dreams, the flashbacks, the mood swings and the insomnia. I thought I was just strengthening my case to go home for the day. I couldn't have cared less what tomorrow would bring.

So that is how I came clean – sitting in an office, talking to a relative stranger, thinking that the only important thing at the time was getting on a train and then locking myself in my flat with a good quantity of booze and cigarettes. I had no idea that I had just cried for help until I sat down and thought about it later. But it was done and that is the only thing that matters now.

I spoke to him for a good hour and had to fill out a questionnaire very similar to one I had filled out soon after the bombings. When all this was done, he told me that he thought I was suffering from post-traumatic stress disorder. I took that with a pinch of salt, of course. I was just interested in the smoking and the drinking that was only 90 minutes away by train. In fact, as the guy was talking to me I was hatching a plot to get some drink from the train station to warm up on before I got home.

He suggested that I go and see a specialist trauma clinic not far from where I was working at the time. It had been set up by the NHS for all the people who had been involved in the bombings, from the emergency services to the victims and their families. I told him that my head had already been 'shrunken' and that I didn't think that it would do any good, but apparently they were using some kind of new desensitisation therapy and it was different to the treatment I had had before. I agreed to go along with it, just to make life easier. If the job saw me making an effort, then I would be able to go back quicker. It was obvious to me at this point that they already thought I was mental, so I needed at least to give them the impression that I was fixed.

I left the office that day on the understanding that I would at least give it a shot and after getting signed off work by my doctor for a while I would report in every now and again to let work know how I was getting on. I felt OK with this, though. I was convinced that all I needed was a break. I hadn't taken any leave for over eight months and I thought that I had simply burned myself out by working so many hours. I'd toe the party line for a few weeks and go back to work refreshed and ready to go.

I think about a week had passed before I got the letter in the post for my first appointment with the traumatic stress clinic. I was surprised at how quickly it had been sorted out, but the sooner the better, as I wasn't doing myself any favours being left to my own devices at home.

Because I didn't have work to distract me, the dreams and flashbacks were getting worse. I had nothing to fill my time and I had too much time to think. I had taken to filling my days up by spending as much time as I could with friends and all of my evenings in the pub getting drunk and passing out when I got home. I hardly spent any time in my flat; it was literally just a place to sleep. I was living on my own and I had nothing to occupy me when I was there. I would find myself daydreaming about my experiences and losing vast amounts of time running over events time and time again in my head. I wasn't eating, I was only sleeping when I was drunk and I was living in squalor, not even bothering to clean up after myself. Sometimes I would snap out of it and have a cleaning spree and not go to the pub for a couple of days, but it wouldn't be long until I slipped again and woke up fully clothed on the sofa with a cigarette burned out between my fingers and a head that felt like it was going to explode.

This was a very bad period for me. I felt like I was treading water. I couldn't work, I wouldn't take the pills that the doctor was prescribing me because they meant I couldn't drink and, whenever I stopped to think, my mind would race back to a point in time when I was immersed in the dark world of that underground tunnel. I could see no end to this feeling and I really was near the point of despair. But then something happened, a bolt out of the blue that would start me on the road to recovery and put the smile back on my face. I could never have expected that at the lowest point of my life I would meet the person I would want to spend the rest of it with.

Chapter Thirty-Two

FLORENCE

It happened when I was on a night out with some friends. For once I wasn't smashed out of my nut, because I was feeling a little rough from the night before. It was a party to celebrate a friend finishing university and we all planned to go into Canterbury and have a good drink and a good dance. I wasn't looking for anything else but having fun and if anyone had told me then that I was going to meet a woman and fall in love that night, I would have laughed in their face. After all, nothing good happened in my life and I had the last ten months to prove it.

Her name is Florence and she is a friend of Lisa, whom I mentioned earlier in the book – the girlfriend of my best mate, Dave. I had met Flo on a few occasions before this night, as she had been going out with an old school friend for a while, but I had never been on a night out with her and could never have guessed that we would hit it off the way that we did.

We didn't have much to do with each other for the first part of the night. Things were pretty tame before the drink started to flow and to tell you the truth I was thinking about making my excuses to leave. I only stayed because everyone was talking about going to a local club for a dance and I am always up for that, as the place is open until the early hours, which meant that I could consume a greater quantity of booze.

When we got to the club, I found myself standing with the blokes at the bar and getting a little bored. They were chatting about the usual shit and as I have said before the things that mattered to me before did not seem to any more, so I wasn't really interested in anything they were saying. I wanted to dance and have some fun, so I went to find the girls.

I found them in the corner near the DJ and they were definitely having more fun than the boys. I found a space with them and started to dance, or at least do something that resembled dancing – it kind of involved shuffling my feet and randomly flailing my arms in no kind of rhythm. Flo cottoned on to this and started making fun of me and mimicking my solid–gold moves. Being the exhibitionist that I am, I started to play up to her and it didn't take long before it seemed like we were the only ones on the dance floor.

I can't remember how long we went on like that for, and to be honest I can't even remember who else was there. All I knew was that I was having the best time that I'd had in ages and this woman had won me over in a very short period of time. When everyone wanted to leave the club, I was very disappointed. I wanted the evening to go on forever. I knew that I wouldn't have the confidence to pursue anything with Flo, I had no self-esteem left and I knew that if I walked away from her then I would never get another chance. But still I did nothing.

On the way to the taxis, I resolved to give it a miss with Flo. I already had enough going on in my life; I really didn't want to subject anyone to what was going on in my head. I put the idea to the back of my mind and continued the evening at a friend's house, where we had all gone for drinks after the club. I was content just to have a good time and forget about my worries for a few hours at least.

At my friend's house, somebody turned on a karaoke machine and I was off. I have a terrible habit of singing when I'm drunk. I just can't help myself, I am the scourge of the karaoke in my mum's pub, handing in ticket after ticket and making my sister, who runs it, rush them to the front of the queue. Anyway, this night I was on form and was challenging everyone to sing-offs and everything – the neighbours must have hated me. But it didn't seem to put Flo off, because when I wasn't wailing like a banshee I found myself deep in conversation with her.

During one of our conversations in the early hours of the morning, I realised something and the realisation stopped me in my tracks: I wasn't thinking about anything else. I was talking to Flo and it could have been like the last year hadn't happened. Since talking to her I had not thought about any of my experiences, I had no nasty images popping into my head and I felt more relaxed than I had in months. I had to see this woman again.

Before the night was over for the pair of us, I had asked for her number and even after the time we had spent together I was still surprised when she gave it to me. I was so happy, I felt like a love-sick teenager and I couldn't wait to see her again. I sent her a text message the next day and my heart was in my mouth waiting for a reply. I loved the feeling – I felt so alive and for me to feel anything but sadness and anger was amazing; I couldn't have been happier. I was beginning to think that if I hadn't had bad luck then I would have had none at all, but now in the space of 24 hours I was on top of the world.

Flo and I saw each other the next day and have seen each other every day since. We are engaged to be married and she makes me very happy. We have had our ups and downs, but when it comes to my state of mind and being understanding about the experiences that I have had, I couldn't ask for anyone more compassionate and caring. I have still never spoken to Flo about what I have been through, but I do not need to. She can sense my moods and does what she can to help me out of them.

I remember one time I came home from work very depressed. I had been to a sudden death at Victoria Underground. An elderly gentleman had had a massive heart attack on the escalator and died in front of me. The paramedics tried to revive him, but it was just his time. There was no blood, no gore, just the passing of someone very quickly and, I hope, painlessly. But it got to me, whereas a year before it wouldn't have. It really upset me to see this man die. I couldn't put the defensive barrier up as I used to – it was very similar to the way I had felt with the young kids in north London. It just seemed that these events were very personal for me, I was getting emotionally attached to them and feeling very strongly, whereas I hadn't ever before. But once one thing got through what defences I had, everything that had ever upset me would come flooding in.

Flo could tell that I wasn't right but she didn't say anything, she left me alone until I was ready to say something. I ran myself a bath and she came into the bathroom and sat on the toilet, talking to me as I tried to relax and come to terms with what I had seen that day. We talked about anything apart from work until I was ready to tell her. For some reason I could open up to her, whereas I had never done it with anyone before.

It was not one of the worst incidents that I had been to by far, but I felt the need to talk to Flo about it because I trusted her. She listened intently to me for a short while and I could see the feeling in her eyes – she wasn't just humouring me, she was actually empathising with me. Then I shocked myself and cried. I couldn't believe it: I could never remember ever crying in front of anyone, but now it seemed OK. Flo reached over and hugged me and I sobbed on her shoulder until I felt better. After that, things were different: I wasn't so upset about my experience, it was if a weight had been lifted off my chest and it felt good. But most important of all, I finally had someone in my life that I felt I could trust. This one was a keeper and my only regret is that I didn't know her and have her in my life a year before; things might have been very different.

Chapter Thirty-Three

HELP AT LAST

The second thing that helped me out came soon after meeting Flo, although I did not know it at the time. I mentioned earlier about the referral to the traumatic stress clinic that the Occupational Health advisor at work had made for me; well, I received a letter through the post from them giving me a date for my first appointment. The letter stated that I had to go for an assessment so they could decide who would be best to treat me – if they decided I needed treating at all.

I made a deal with myself at this stage that I was going to go along with it. It was clear to me by now that I needed help and I could not deal with the issues in my head on my own. I had to swallow my stupid pride and get myself fixed. I think now that it was my budding relationship with Flo that motivated me, not anything else. We had been getting on like a house on fire, but when things got on top of me and I got stressed, all the negative things started to creep into my mind and this made me a difficult person to be around at times. I was finally happy for the first time in years and I wasn't going to let that slip away because of my stupid male pride.

The first appointment that I had was a bit of a disappointment for me. I do not know what I expected, but I wasn't helping, no matter what promises I had made myself. I sat in a room and the woman who had been assigned to assess me asked me the same sort of questions that I had been asked directly after the bombings by the woman who had done my first assessment nearly a year earlier. But to my surprise, I found myself treating this woman exactly the same way that I had the last one. I lied to her. I completely shut her out and hated myself as I was doing it. I wasn't trying to fool her like I was the previous time, because now I really wanted help, but I couldn't help it. Something that I did not understand was preventing me from letting anyone in.

I sat there at the end of the hour and was thinking to myself that I had blown it. I wanted to start again, I wanted the hour over so that I could start from the beginning and tell this woman what was really going on in my head, but that wasn't going to happen. As we were wrapping up, I was waiting for her to say that she didn't think that there was anything wrong with me and that I could go back to work now, that I'd rested for a couple of weeks. But that didn't happen. Somehow she had seen though my act and told me to come back in a week and we would start something that she called desensitisation therapy. I was ecstatic on the inside, but I didn't show it: now I could concentrate on getting my life back on track, but only if this worked. I hadn't had too much joy with the last shrink I had seen.

As it turned out, later my therapist told me that desensitisation therapy was the only way that I could be treated. She said that I had the stuff so deeply buried and I was so reluctant to talk about it that this method was the only one that could conceivably help me. I am so glad this woman knew her stuff, because she had picked up on what others had missed: without her help, I dread to think what would have become of me; I was already in self-destruct mode. How long would it have been before I let my issues get the better of me and destroyed my new relationship?

I turned up for my first appointment and was met by the same woman as before. She explained to me what the treatment I was going to receive would entail. In short, she was going to sit me down in a room for 90 minutes a week and make me think about my experiences on 7 July 2005. I didn't have to talk about them as experiences, but I was to visualise them in my head in as much detail as I possibly could. As well as this, I was to learn relaxation techniques to learn to focus when it all got a bit much and to chill me out when I had finished a particularly upsetting session.

My relaxation technique was to think about fishing. I love to fish and try and go whenever I can. If I have something going on in my life that is stressful and I don't want to think about it, or I want to relax and put things in perspective, I go fishing. It's a fantastic form of relaxation: you can sit there and think about nothing apart from what you are doing then and there, or you can do it on autopilot and think about your life and your problems as much as you want. I have found it very helpful all through my life, even if it has just been a little bit of down time to get together.

To relax, I used to imagine myself sitting by the side of a lake in the summer with my shirt off. I am surrounded by reeds, looking out onto the flat, calm water. I can hear insects buzzing quietly all around me and I can feel the warmth of the sun on my back and my neck. There is no one else around and all I have to concentrate on is the tip of the float sitting perfectly still on the surface of the water. I create this image in my head and I am at peace.

Before I continue, I'll quickly explain what desensitisation therapy is. It is a really interesting subject in its own right, but a brief summary will also help you understand how upsetting the sessions were and how it helped me. I have explained how the human brain stores information that it takes in during a traumatic event. It stores it as a big mess of jumbled-up images and sensory perceptions and then, in an effort to sort it all out and understand it, the brain relives the event through bad dreams and flashbacks, all the symptoms that I had been displaying over the last ten months or so. This type of therapy allows your brain to sort through this information in a controlled way so that it can be stored it away without putting you under too much stress.

Consciously thinking about the event in question over and over again helps you to organise everything, and the more you do it the better things get. As more information gets sorted, the less you have the involuntary reactions to triggers that you encounter. The theory is that you are always going to have the memories, but you are not going to be too traumatised when you remember them. It is ingenious stuff and helpful for people like me who are a little emotionally repressed.

The first sessions that I attended were the worst. I had deliberately avoided thinking about any of my experiences on that day and it was horrific to concentrate on them intentionally and think about everything in as much detail as I could. In essence, I was doing the exact opposite to what I had been conditioning myself to do in the months that had passed. I was also very surprised that as well as seeing the images in my head I was also feeling what I had felt at the time. It was as if my brain had remembered everything from what I saw and what I felt, both emotionally and physically.

During these initial sessions, I was a bit of a mess. I experienced the full spectrum of emotions, from being reduced to tears of sadness to tears of anger. It was a very disturbing and difficult time. My therapist would tell me to relax and let my mind go where it wanted and I would find myself standing in the tunnel staring at some horror that I hadn't thought about since the day. I had buried all of it so deeply that in nearly every session I would remember something new that I had blocked out because the image or the emotion was too upsetting.

I used to leave these sessions in a serious state sometimes. I would keep as brave a face as I could during the sessions, but after I'd left the building I would try and find somewhere quiet for a while so I could collect myself before I went home. During those first few times, I was convinced things were actually getting worse, but I now know that this was only because I was experiencing new memories that I had not been forced to deal with at the time.

As I attended more and more of these sessions, however, I slowly started to notice things getting better. The nightmares were getting less frequent and I would not have as many flashbacks or waking dreams as I had before. During my time with the therapist, I was chronologically working my way through the events and found that I could actually think about some of the things from the day and not get freaked out by them. It was a slow progress, but I cannot describe the relief that I felt because of this. After so long, things were finally starting to happen in a positive way.

Even though the sessions were helping me, on the whole I still found that I was holding a lot back, even from myself. There were some things that were just too painful to think about, things that I didn't understand and things that I didn't want to see in my head. My mind would wander on to these subjects and immediately I would push them away and think about something completely unrelated. One minute I would be crouched in the tunnel with my head in my hands feeling absolute despair that I couldn't think of a way to get Gill out of the tunnel, then my mind would push that image away and I would be sitting by the side of a lake, fishing, trying to relax and forget about my worries for just a little while.

Because the sessions were so hard on me, it was having a negative impact on my relationship with Flo. I was very grumpy when I used to come home and was quite difficult to be around a lot of the time. One thing has always amazed me about her, though: there is no way she can understand what my colleagues and I went through that day, but she is always there to prop me up when I am down and she has a lot of tolerance when it comes to my issues surrounding that event. I was stunned by this, because even though we had only been together for a short period of time, she still showed extraordinary patience and compassion to me. Looking back, I contribute a large part of my recovery to her, although I have never told her that to her face.

As time went on, I found the sessions easier to go to and even though it was still very difficult to think about the details of the event I could feel the progress that I was making every time I went. I had worked through a lot of very disturbing stuff, but I was finding the emotions that I felt at the time a lot more difficult to come to terms with than what I actually saw. For instance, every time I thought about certain things, I would get an overwhelming sense of inadequacy and failure. You may find this difficult to understand, but most of it centred on Gill's rescue. I had been avoiding thinking about this in the previous sessions that I had attended because it provoked the strongest reactions from me.

I couldn't understand why I felt this way until it was explained to me in one of the sessions. You see, I had thought that Gill had died after all our efforts in that godforsaken tunnel. I was under the impression that I had failed despite all my attempts and every time I thought about her I would experience those negative emotions regardless of how things turned out. I found this exceptionally hard to deal with and this was at the root of the problem when it came to having a friendship with Gill. I couldn't help feeling this way when I was around her, but because I couldn't control it I had avoided seeing her properly since the episode that I had experienced during the wedding. I had spoken to her on the phone and seen her for short periods but that was it. It just upset me too much and it was torture not understanding why.

I find it very hard to explain how I could have felt the guilt I did over someone's death when she was actually alive. It was disturbing and I would have gone on not understanding it and carrying on the way I did if it wasn't for the treatment that I received. The therapy forced me to deal with this and face up to it. The advisor I was seeing would ask me to tell her what I was feeling when I thought about my time in the tunnel with Gill. She would then ask me why I was feeling that way and then she would explain why I shouldn't have those feelings and what I should actually be feeling. Eventually it started to sink in, but it was hard work even to make a start, as my emotions were so deeply engrained.

The best example of this were the feelings that I got when I realised that I couldn't carry Gill through that tunnel any more. I felt so guilty because the way my mind interpreted it was that I was weak for not being able to carry on, and that she had died because of my weakness. The simple fact that she had lived was irrelevant when I was in that dark place. My irrational mind was not thinking about the fact that

Gill's injuries were making it nigh-on impossible to get a decent grip on her, or the fact that the blood that I was covered in was making her slip off my shoulder, or the fact that when I tried to carry her she screamed in pain. There was even a point when I thought that having her over my shoulder and making her scream that much was the reason that she had ultimately died.

I know now that I didn't have a choice in what I did and I know that our efforts saved her life, but you could not have told me that at the time. It was only when I had it broken down and explained to me that I finally understood, but when I did it was almost like having a cold, refreshing shower after working on a humid day. When I came out of the other side, it was like washing all of those issues off me and feeling refreshed.

As time went on I could feel that things were improving and by the time the anniversary of the bombings came round I was feeling a hell of a lot better. But as things started appearing on the news about the bombings, I started to relapse again. My therapist told me that this was completely normal and that I should just carry on doing what I was doing until it was over. I had already made the decision that I was going to hide for the day anyway; I didn't see the point in exposing myself to any unnecessary anguish.

The day came round and I had made sure that I had an appointment scheduled. I had a feeling that I'd want to talk about some stuff and thought it would help. Gill had invited me to a church service and I knew that some of the other guys were going, but I didn't fancy it. I wanted to, out of respect for those that had lost their lives, but I didn't think that I was ready for stuff like that and I still was a bit dodgy about seeing Gill.

I went to my appointment that day but I had physically to drag myself into London to do it. During my session we talked mainly about the event but we didn't go into as much detail as we had before – I think it was pretty obvious that I was having a tough time of it that day. As I had been on my way to the session, I had experienced my first flashback in weeks, though when I spoke about it I was assured that it was normal given all the emotions that were being stirred up. But mostly in that ninety minutes we spoke about Gill, as I had been having quite a bit of contact with her over the phone – we talked about the things that she had been doing and what she had arranged for the day of the anniversary. I had come to the conclusion that I wanted to see more of her and asked my therapist to help me in achieving this.

As for the rest of the anniversary, I simply went home and got stupidly drunk with Flo. We didn't talk about the events of the previous year, just about her hopes for the future. The day passed by like any other and I couldn't have been happier with that. I do not know what I would have done without Flo.

Chapter Thirty-Four

A FRIEND FOR LIFE

My relationship with Gill had been a continuous problem for me since the time I found out that she was alive. It was clear that Gill wanted me in her life – she was always making steps to contact me and build a relationship, but I felt at the time that it was something that I couldn't give her, no matter how much I wanted to. I had popped into her place of work on occasion and had been to her house once or twice, but that was it. She made me feel weak because of the emotions that she stirred up in me and it seemed like I couldn't control what was going on in my head when I was with her.

I had been working really hard in the therapy sessions to tackle the issues that I had been left with after the event and had even taken to subjecting myself to the memories outside the sessions because I could see that the technique was working. It was still taking a lot out of me, but because of the improvement that I could see in myself I was keen to get better as soon as I possibly could. Things were going well with Flo, the treatment was working and I was getting ready to go back to work. Everything, on the whole, was starting to look up for me. The only thing that I had left to make a start on was Gill: I wanted to have more to do with her and I realised that if I could get over the rest of the stuff that was bothering me I could certainly do this.

My therapist and I had been talking about Gill in great detail. I had identified it as something that I was really having trouble getting over and she told me that we would concentrate on this area as much as we could in the forthcoming sessions that we had booked. I felt as if this was one of the last things that I needed to get sorted in my head, as well as the most important. Gill was the biggest thing that had happened to me on the day and I couldn't help but think that most of my problems were centred around her. Also, I felt that I had a connection with this woman, she was in my thoughts for a lot of the time and I wanted to explore the extent of our relationship. Would we just be acquaintances, or would we be friends?

I am not sure how many sessions I attended after that; we had bounced around the subject of Gill time and time again, but for some reason I still couldn't bring myself to talk about her in any great detail, it was just too upsetting. I had seen her occasionally and was still speaking to her on the phone, but things were still difficult. I just couldn't seem to get past it. The situation was very frustrating, because I felt that I was making good progress in all the other areas. The bad dreams had just about stopped and I was getting the first unbroken night's sleep that I had had for as long as I could remember.

One day, at the end of one of the sessions that I was having, I promised my therapist that I would really try to work on the subject the next time I was in. But as I left the building I suddenly said to myself, 'Screw it I'm gong to see her.' I phoned Gill from outside Goodge Street Underground, made sure she was in and then made my way to north London, where she lives.

When I arrived at Gill's house, she was the only one in and for that I was a little thankful. It was she that I wanted to speak to; I thought that if I could be truthful with her then maybe I could get some of the stuff off my chest that had been crippling me for so long. Gill greeted me with her customary long hug that always had felt a little awkward before but now felt like kind of a relief. This was about the first time that we had been on our own together and it was nice to know that she didn't feel as uneasy as I did. Hopefully, I could draw some strength from that and tell her what I came there to do.

We sat at the kitchen table and Gill made me a fantastic cup of coffee. I wanted to help her, as she was walking with the aid of her stick, but I was amazed at how proficiently she was getting around and how she was making the everyday tasks that we all take for granted look easy despite the fact that she was having to manage without her legs. I already had an endless amount of respect for this woman, but just seeing her function like this added to it tenfold.

At last we sat down to talk. Gill was sitting at the head of the table and I was to her right. We started chatting about life in general, what we had both been up to, but I felt like I was boxing around the real reason why I was there. I think now that I needed reassurance from her. I needed to hear it from her in person that I did everything I could and that I had not failed her on the day. I wanted her to tell me that I had no reason to put myself through the pain any more, but even as I was sitting there, looking at her face, I was still feeling it. As hard as it is to understand, I felt like a failure in her presence.

Eventually, we started talking about the events of 7 July. It was the natural progression of the conversation that we were having and before I realised it we were talking about our own experiences from that day. I told her about the struggle that we had getting her out, about the broken stretcher and me not being able to carry her on my shoulder. In turn, she was telling me how the only things that she could remember from the tunnel itself were the sound of my voice and my holding her hand. That was the breaking point for me and I started to cry much as I am now as I am writing about it. I couldn't hold it back any more; I could feel the release just by talking to her. I didn't sob like I have done on my own, but I couldn't stop the tears from spilling down my cheeks. I could see that she was also on the verge of crying as well and we both sat there feeling the same connection that I knew was there all along.

We spoke for ages about everything that we could remember about that day. I think that this was the first time that Gill had heard the full story of what transpired in that tunnel. Out of everyone there, I think that I was the only one who had been with her from the time we found her in the train to when we left her with the medics in the booking hall. I think that she knew that anyway, without my telling her a thing. I had felt a definite connection with her that day, and as I have said before, I would have given my life in her place without a second thought. Gill's rescue that day consumed every ounce of my strength, emotionally as well as physically, and had haunted my dreams – both unconscious and waking – for a year or more. It was such a relief to be sitting in the same room with her on this day; it was as if sharing my feelings with her and talking to her about them in person was washing away all the guilt that I had been keeping locked inside me for so long. She just seemed more real.

I would love to explain to you why I felt such a connection with Gill or the reasons why it helped me so much just to sit down and talk to her, sharing our pain and fears left over from the day – but the truth is that I can't. I could never explain why Gill is so important to me now and why she had been the main source of my anguish in the past, as I do not understand it myself. I never intentionally set out to have a friendship with her, but the more I think about it the more I am convinced that I didn't have a choice. If I have learnt anything from that dark day, it is that things happen for a reason and some things are just meant to be. I was meant to be with Gill during her ordeal and I was meant to care about her as much as I did. We all were – I have spoken to the other lads that were involved in her rescue and we are all in agreement that there is something special about her.

Gill and I sat in her flat and talked for several hours. There were more tears, but more importantly there was laughter as well. We got to know each other on a more personal level, each finding out where the other had come from and what had led to us both being in London that day. But whereas I had always felt under a strain talking to Gill in the past, this time I felt at ease — it was as if we had knew each other already, but knew nothing about each other. Again, I know that doesn't make sense, but without being with me on that day I think it would be impossible to explain.

At last it was time for me to leave. I needed to get back home to meet Flo and it would take me over two hours to get back; besides, I was feeling exhausted after discussing so many subjects that were surrounded by very deep emotions, not just for me but for Gill as well. I stood to leave and Gill stood with me. She walked me to the top of the stairs and I remember looking at her face and suddenly realising that it was just her face that I was looking at, in the here and now. There was no soot, there was no blood or singed hair, it was just a woman standing in front of me, a woman that I knew would be my friend for life. Gill and I hugged standing at the top of the stairs and we seemed to be stuck there for ages. It was as if this was the first time she had seemed real to me, the first time she had seemed like a normal person and not a symbol of my pain and anguish. Then, when one of her tears rolled down my neck, I realised that this part of my journey was over. Gill was now part of my life and that would never change.

Since that day, our relationship has grown more than I could have possibly hoped. It was Gill who encouraged me to write my feelings down on paper – and that, of course, led to this book. I speak to her nearly every day on the phone, more so lately as she is always in my thoughts. I try and see her as much as I can and she is always there for me when I need a friend to discuss things with. Our relationship has developed beyond the events of that day into so much more. Although we still discuss the issues surrounding terrorism and politics, we also talk about what is going on in our lives as well. She is always there when I need someone to talk to and I can honestly say, with my hand on my heart, that she is the only person that I have met in my life that I feel that I can open up to completely. I have never trusted anyone as much with my feelings or my fears.

I like to think now that we would have met regardless of the events of July 2005. I cannot believe that someone who I have become so close to would have never entered my life if one event had not have happened. But perhaps we were meant to meet that way; perhaps the experience that has changed both of our lives has laid the foundation for something else. I am not a religious man, or a superstitious one, but perhaps the people who we were before the bombings could not have been friends. We have changed so much as people because of that event. Perhaps it is only now that we are capable of being such a big part of each other's lives.

Chapter ThirtyFive

THINGS DON'T FIT ANY MORE

Now I have finished my sessions with the counsellor and I am back to work, I am struggling to take stock of my life as I find it. I have come out of the other side of my ordeal, but things are not as I expected them to be. I do not recognise my life any more and I do not recognise myself as a person either. When I was concentrating on getting better and sorting my head out, I didn't notice the changes. Now I am trying to evaluate the position that I am in, those changes are staring me in the face and I am not sure if I like what I see.

It is as if the things that mattered to me so much before I started on this journey have become insignificant and have been replaced by things that I am struggling to understand. It feels as though I have a completely new take on life, but although I know about the things that do not matter, I am struggling to find the things that do. Before the bombings, I felt that I had direction and ambition, but even though I still possess both of those characteristics, I do not know what I am driven about and I do not know what my ambitions are.

The people that I need in my life have changed as well. Although I still value the friends that I had before the event, I do not see them nearly as much as I used to. I do not think that they understand me as they used to and that I am a different person to them as well as myself. The only people that fit into my life comfortably now are people that I have met since 7 July 2005. These people have only known me as I am now and I think that is the reason why they fit as they do. Of course, the most important people that I have now are Flo and Gill. I think above all other people they understand me the most and are the people who have given me the most support though all my troubles, whether they know it or not.

Work has come as the biggest shock to me. I might sound like a bit of a weirdo for saying this, but before all this started, my job was my life. I actually used to look forward to going to work and never struggled to get out of bed to start a shift; I was thought of as a keen and competent officer and I enjoyed people's opinion of me. It seemed that I had found my calling in life, a career that I could enjoy and stick with for the long term. I was convinced that this would never change; nothing that I had encountered in my job before had ever even come close to changing my mind on that.

Now, I am not so sure and all the things that I thought were set in stone before have changed. Since going back, I have struggled to apply myself as I used to, but I do not seem to be able to find the same passion for it any more. I have tried and tried, but it seems that no matter what I do I always end up making mistakes – not big ones, but little ones that on the whole add up to a major problem.

I am still enjoying the practical side of things and am never happier than when I am out and about in the car, meeting people and dealing with incidents first hand. That is one place that I do not make mistakes, because it matters there and then and I am forced to apply myself to whatever I am dealing with. That part of the job, at least, still comes very naturally to me.

It is the office-based side of the work that lets me down now. I just do not seem to be able to concentrate on it and unfortunately it is a big part of what a police officer needs to do in this day and age. Behind every person that we arrest there is a mountain of paperwork involved – it is a critical part of the job and my proficiency in that area has been lacking of late. My mind just wanders uncontrollably; I can't help it. It always seems like there is something more important to do. I only feel like I am engaged in something worthwhile when I am actually doing something practical and to tell you the truth I do not even feel like that is enough sometimes; I always feel as if I should be doing something more. I feel a nearly uncontrollable urge to make a difference to the world that we live in, but I am not nearly naïve enough to think that I can.

When I was at my lowest, all I wanted was for things to go back to the way they were. I wished that the event that had put me through a living hell had not happened and that I could be back in the life that I had before. I even remember saying to Gill one of the first times I met her that I would be happy and have all the thanks I would ever need from her if I could just see her return to the normal life that she had before getting on the Tube that day. But now I am not too sure for either of us. I have accepted that things will never be the same again and even though I am struggling to find my place in life I am excited about the future. The unknown is daunting, but my future is mine to mould now, whereas before I was living as a result of the consequences of my past.

It wouldn't be right to say that I have become a recluse, but I do like to spend a lot of time on my own, whereas before I used to surround myself with people. I do not think of it as unhealthy, as it might do from the outside looking in, as I would someone else's life. But what you have to consider is that I have a lot to think about now and I have a lot to plan. I need to work out who I am and what I want to do with my life; it is like being a teenager again – and if I want to lock myself in my room and listen to heavy metal, I will!

Joking aside, although this is a period of self-discovery for me, I have an entirely different take on just about everything. I react so differently to the way I used to, it is like my emotions are wired in a completely new way. I am so much more open than I used to be. Whereas before I never used to talk to anyone, I now have several people that I trust and can rely on when it comes to matters of personal importance. The events of the last year have been the catalysts that have given me the chance to change things and because of them I have had the opportunity to discover so much.

I never would have found that I had a passion for writing as I have done through all of this; I would never have met Gill and I probably wouldn't have met Flo. These are all massive parts of my life now and I owe them all to this second chance I have been given. I now have the chance not to start again with a clean canvas, but at least to paint over it with whatever I want.

When I think about my future, I see nothing but options and opportunity. I still plan to stay in the Transport Police, as they have been very good to me over the course of my career, and I hope I can find a place with them where I feel like I fit. I still love the job, but I feel I need to be in a different role. I am based in a control room at the moment, but that is not exactly working out for me. I feel claustrophobic being in an office all the time and I am itching to be out on the ground, getting my hands dirty.

In my personal life, I am happier than I have been for a very long time, now I can appreciate what is important to me emotionally as well as practically. It has not been an easy ride, because I have been struggling with my emotions and I have been forced to deal with a lot of situations that I have not been exposed to before. But for the first time I can remember, I have hope for the future. Flo and I plan to take a few months out next year to go travelling and we both hope that this will give us the chance to evaluate our lives and figure out what we want to do with our future. At present, we plan to get married when we get back and build a life together. But, whatever we decide to do, I know I will be happy with her at my side.

Gill and I will remain friends for the rest of our lives. We share something that cannot be put into words and I do not even want to try to do so. We have both come out of a very dark place both physically and mentally and have gained an understanding between each other that is more precious to me than just about anything else. She is in my thoughts every day.

★ ★ ★ ★ ★

I find myself feeling a little sad now I am coming to the end of this book. It has helped me so much to express my feelings in the way that I have in these pages. I have been through a journey and now I am nearing its completion. Writing this has made me laugh, it has made me cry and it has made me look inside myself on countless occasions. It has helped me to understand some of what I have been feeling and work out some of the issues in my life, a lot of which have nothing to do with the bombings.

I think that even though I am a different person, I am a better person, and I hope that I can find my path in life. I hope that I can find something that gives my life the extra meaning that I am searching for. Perhaps I will find it when I am travelling, or in my new life with Flo, but I am sure it is out there for me somewhere. More than anything now, I want to be at peace and I am sure that when I find that illusive something I will be.

When I think back to that day in July 2005 – and the images of the destruction that was caused – it still upsets me, but not in the way that it used to. I have accepted that I cannot forget those horrible things, as much as I tried to in the past. They are part of me now and will be for the rest of my life. All I can do now is try and be as positive about the future as I can and draw on my experiences for strength. I am proud of what we achieved on that day. Everyone involved did all they could to the best of their ability and as a whole we took chaos and turned it into order. We did all anyone could have possibly asked of us, and if I have nothing else in life, I will always have that.

AUTHOR'S NOTE

I hope now you have read what is contained in these pages you understand better what was experienced that day by so many people, and have understood the points that I wanted to put across about the effects of trauma on the human mind after an event such as the 7 July bombings.

I am very anxious about how people perceive me and what I have written. Now that I know that my thoughts and experiences are going to be published, I find myself torn between wanting to keep this locked up inside and making my account public. On numerous occasions in this book I have mentioned what a private person I am and I find it ironic that the first time I talk in any detail about my experiences many people are going to read about them.

You now know me nearly as well as I know myself, but after a lot of soul-searching I think that leaving myself so exposed is a small price to pay for telling this story. I believe with every fibre of my being that I needed to say what I have and raise the points that I feel so strongly about.

You have now had a very personal insight into the innermost reaches of my soul; you have shared my hopes, my fears, my pain and my misery. You have seen me at my highest and my lowest. I have given this book everything I can to make it as powerful as possible. Anything less would not have done the event the justice it deserves.

My life seems a little empty now that writing this is over. It has been a great healing tool for me and has done me more good than any therapy I have received. I can never thank Gill Hicks and her husband Joe enough for encouraging and inspiring me throughout the whole process. If it were not for them, I would never have even thought of writing this book and would still have all this locked up inside of me.

Gill and I have become great friends – in fact, we are more than that and I do not possess the vocabulary to describe what we have. That is why I want to dedicate this book to her and Flo. Both of these wonderful women have given me so much support and love when I have not had the strength on my own. Most of the time they did not even realise what they were doing and that is what makes them so special. They have changed my life and made it a better place to live. Wherever I end up in the future, I will always have that and I cannot thank them enough for it.

I feel like a new person now and for the first time in as long as I can remember I am looking forward to the future.

I do not know what I will do or where I will be, but that is what is so good about it. I am excited, and that is a fantastic feeling. After finishing this book, I think that I may be a writer. I was told once that what you think about when you first wake up in the morning is what you are meant to do with your life. I do not think I would make a very good adult-movie star, though, so I might go for the second thing I think about: writing.

Thank you for sharing this experience with me. I hope, above all else, that at least one small part of what I have written has touched each one of you in a positive way. That would make all of this worthwhile for me.

AFTERWORD
by GILL HICKS

I start each day by thanking every one of those brave and remarkable people who did everything humanly possible on 7 July 2005 to save my life, who risked their own lives to do so and who never gave up on me. I owe them everything – every day that I have had, every joy, every tear, every smile and laugh, every bit of life that I have enjoyed I credit to them. The depth of my gratitude is immeasurable.

In a breath, my world changed; in the time it took to click your fingers the world had changed forever for all of us in that carriage on that morning. I was engulfed by a thick blackness: I couldn't see, I couldn't breathe, I couldn't feel my body. My only thoughts were of death, that what I was experiencing was my death, my end. I started to lose consciousness, hearing only the muffled screams of my fellow commuters.

My greatest fear – that of dying alone – was being realised.

I woke to find myself sitting on a bench seat in the carriage. It was eerily quiet. I didn't know what had happened, I didn't know a bomb had exploded; actually I didn't know or think about anything except trying to survive. I couldn't feel anything, I couldn't feel any of my body. The thick black smoke had lifted to a thinner grey, revealing the horror of my situation. I could see both my legs, or what resembled my legs. I was losing a lot of blood and my eyes were desperate to shut and never open again. It took every ounce of strength to fight the calling of death, to stay awake and wait for rescue – I knew the rescuers would come and save us, I just had to stay strong, to hold on.

I saw a torch and heard the two best words in the English language: Priority One. They were here, I was going to be rescued, they would get me out; I surrendered my body completely to them.

I was cold, ice cold – I'd lost over 50 per cent of my blood by this stage. I could sense the difficulty that the rescuers were having in getting me out of the tangled wreck of the carriage and down the tunnel. I was fading in and out, hovering above death.

One man held my hand; his clasp filled me with warmth. I could hear his voice urging me to stay with him, each plea more urgent than the last. I felt connected to him – somehow his grip was keeping me alive. It was as if he was giving me a piece of himself. I felt safe, I felt loved, it was calming for me to know that, if I was to die in that moment, I would die in the arms of someone who cared for me, someone who was prepared to give his own life to save mine; I wasn't alone.

It was Aaron who held my hand that morning.

Aaron and I share a unique bond – we are bound by unconditional love, a special and rare connection that I am sure will last a lifetime. He has become a treasured friend, someone for whom I have great respect and admiration. Aaron has the most enormous heart and the most wonderful spirit. We shared a hell that fortunately only a few people know or understand, but the beauty of our relationship is that it's not defined by tragedy.

He represents everything that is good about life and humanity.

Gill xxx